A PRIMER ON THE HISTORY AND PHILSOPHY OF EDUCATION

Mark Mraz

University Press of America,® Inc.
Lanham · Boulder · New York · Toronto · Plymouth, UK

LA205
.M73
2010
c.6

Copyright © 2010 by
University Press of America,® Inc.
4501 Forbes Boulevard
Suite 200
Lanham, Maryland 20706
UPA Acquisitions Department (301) 459-3366

Estover Road
Plymouth PL6 7PY
United Kingdom

All rights reserved
Printed in the United States of America
British Library Cataloging in Publication Information Available

Library of Congress Control Number: 2010924015
ISBN: 978-0-7618-5119-6 (paperback : alk. paper)
eISBN: 978-0-7618-5120-2

⊖™ The paper used in this publication meets the minimum
requirements of American National Standard for Information
Sciences—Permanence of Paper for Printed Library Materials,
ANSI Z39.48-1992

Dedicated to my wife Sue, and my daughters Rose and Leah

Thanks to Sue Mraz for editing the book and also a special thanks to Rose Mraz and Scott Hoffman for initially editing and formatting the book.

Contents

Foreword

Dr. Mark Mraz reminds readers that to not understand history is to reject Western Civilization. Undoubtedly, this book is needed at a time when so many of the nation's universities are dropping Western Civilization coursework requirements (e.g. The University of Chicago, 2002). It is poignant that during a time when people are confusing the popular fiction of "The Da Vinci Code" with actual history, this book circumscribes an outline of "Great" thinkers and gives readers an overview of the history and philosophy of education. Undoubtedly, the material in this book is essential for preservice teachers so that they can begin to understand the foundations of education and its philosophical roots .

Dr. Edwin P. Christmann, Ph.D.
Professor and Chairman, SEFE

Preface

This book is titled *A Primer on the History & Philosophy of Education*. According to Webster's dictionary, a primer is a small introductory book on a subject. This work is exactly that a bare bones basic narrative of the foundational educational history of the American system. It is hoped that the narrative will stimulate both student and teacher to find deeper veins of historical understanding in other works, internet sources, classical texts, and stimulating class discussions. In addition, the brevity of the text allows the instructor to select various paperbacks from primary educational theorists such as Plato, Rousseau, Burke, and Dewey, to augment the course content and tie the books together with lectures and this narrative.

Historically, since the time of the Greeks and Romans one of the key missions of education has always been the cultivation of the good citizen. The whole history of education can be viewed as an attempt at the cultural transmission of this paradigm.

The author tries to present the history of education as a part of the larger picture of the development of civilization. According to Ellwood Cubberley, the eminent educational historian, the history of education should be explained not as an isolated area of study but as a phase of the larger prototype of the progress and process of civilization. Therefore, using the Cubberley model, the historic antecedents of our current education system are explained.

In doing this, it will be necessary to concentrate on the major epochs of civilization which have impacted our current pedagogy. Starting with an overview of history and philosophy, the author proceeds to the Western experience in education as the baseline of all educational eras in the United States.

Mark Mraz, PhD
Slippery Rock, Pennsylvania, 2010

Chapter 1
History & Philosophy

Explain the significance of:

People: Jean Piaget, Marcus Quintilian, Charles Darwin, Johann H. Pestalozzi, Plato, Aristotle, St. Thomas Aquinas, William James, John Dewey, Soren Kierkagaard, Robert Maynard Hutchins, Arthur Bestor, Henry Giroux, Paulo Freire, Harold Rugg, George Counts, Theodore Brameld

Terms: Clio, history, 1859, expanding horizons, circles of love, epistemology, metaphysics, axiology, neo-thomism, existentialism, perennialism, essentialism, progressivism, social reconstructionists, postmodernism

What is History?

Clio, the muse of history, writes on her tablet the deeds of the past. This is how history was made according to the Ancient Greeks. All history is a record of what people have done in the past. Teachers and schools also have a past that can be studied and explored for its own sake. In a broader sense educational history can illuminate the present by allowing current practitioners to build on previous achievements in the field.

Cyclical Nature of History

History as a field of study began with the Classical Greeks. There are many theories of history that historians draw on to explain their craft. Many scholars believe in the cyclical nature of history and there is evidence of this theory in education. A good example of this would be Piaget's Theory of Intellectual Development published in the early part of the Twentieth Century. Educational psychologists explain the sequential developmental stage theory as if it were a modern phenomenon of the 20th Century when in reality, Quintilian, the Roman educator, wrote about it and practiced sequential learning pedagogy in 69 AD. One wonders if Piaget read Quintilian.

Generally speaking, the history of education can be seen as the chronicle of the intellectual development of civilization. From 500 BC until 1859 AD, the world was explained in terms of philosophy and theology. Thinkers such as Socrates, Plato, Quintilian, Aquinas, and Augustine were the frontier scholars in these areas. After 1859, Darwin, Freud, Spencer, and Dewey, to name a few, explained the world in terms of science. These cutting-edge scholars applied science to all fields of knowledge. What happened in 1859 to change the paradigms by which the learned arrived at knowledge?

The Impact of Darwin

In *The Origin of the Species*, Darwin used science to explain the evolution of living things. After this time, the cult of science was used to define the world rather than philosophy or theology. These changes in thought would also alter the principles of teaching and learning. After 1859 AD, epistemology, the philosophy that studies the nature of human knowledge, was altered. This change in turn transformed what was taught and learned. Scholars reasoned that science and the scientific method could be used to teach and learn any academic subject.

The Value of History

Does history have a use value for society? Many historians believe it does. Do some believe it does not? Who really knows? Nonetheless, educational history can be of value to the practicing teacher. He or she can look at the best teaching techniques of the past and apply them to the present. For example, a study of the pedagogy of the Swiss reform educator Johann Pestalozzi would reveal an interesting link to modern curriculum. The typical curriculum in social studies at the primary level, "The Expanding Horizons Curriculum," starts with family, and neighborhood, and then gradually expands to associations farther away in place and time. This curricular manifestation is Pestalozzian in nature and quite similar to his paradigm of the "Circles of Love," in which learning proceeds from family to community and eventually to the world. In practical application of previous pedagogy, the history of education has a use value to teachers.

What is Philosophy?

Philosophy comes from two Greek words "*philo*" and "*sophie*" meaning lover of wisdom. One can say that philosophy is the pursuit of truth by intellectual means and also a system of inquiry. The field is based on fundamental assumptions, logical reasoning, and empirical research.

The Use Value of Philosophy

A philosophy is also a guide for conduct and procedures in a discipline such as education. As a teacher grows professionally, his or her teaching philosophy usually changes from liberal to conservative over their 35 or more years in the classroom.

The Fields of Study in Philosophy

Philosophy is divided into three fields or branches. The first branch, metaphysics, is the field of philosophy that deals with reality. It seeks to answer the question: "What is reality?" Epistemology is the second area, which asks the question: "What is the nature of knowledge?" Most teachers are concerned with epistemology because it determines the knowledge that is eventually taught in the classroom. Lastly, the third sphere is axiology, which is concerned with values and beauty.

Traditional Philosophy

Modern educational theories are grounded in the traditional philosophies of idealism, realism, neo-thomism, pragmatism, and existentialism. The Greek philosopher Plato developed idealism. He believed that reality was in the realm of ideas. Therefore, Plato contended that learning and teaching were intellectual not social or technical.

Aristotle developed realism. He believed that reality existed in the real world and was social.

St. Thomas Aquinas developed neo-thomism. Essentially, Aquinas believed that the ultimate relationship was with God, and the teachers' role was to get the students to God.

William James and John Dewey developed pragmatism. Pragmatism is the only purely American philosophy. The real world and the solution to problems are of concern to the pragmatist. These thinkers believe that truth is relative and whatever works is right. This premise manifests itself in an ever-changing curriculum depending on the current world situation.

Lastly, Soren Kierkagaard developed existentialism. Existentialist theorists believe that "all is nothing." Once a person accepts this, he or she can find the essence in him or herself. Existentialists choose to study things not generally in the curriculum to give voice to underrepresented groups. All of these theories differ in educational goals, curriculum, and teaching methods.

These philosophies have all made an impact on contemporary instructive ideas. Theoretically and historically these five paradigms will be studied in their historical context as well as their modern applications.

Modern Theories of Education

The major modern theories of education are perennialism, essentialism, progressivism, postmodernism, and social reconstructionism. Perennialism is based on platonic idealism. Robert Maynard Hutchins, a past president of the University of Chicago who eliminated college sports because they interfered with academics, was the major proponent of this pedagogical theory. The perennialist's curriculum does not have to be of any utilitarian value. The enduring ideas of Western civilization and Christian doctrine are the major curricular underpinning of this theory.

Essentialism is based on Aristotelian realism. Arthur Bestor, a history professor from the University of Illinois, was the major proponent of this school of thought. The curriculum for the essentialist must be useful or practical. The essentialist paradigm must pertain to real world applications.

Real world applications are also at the heart of progressivism. Progressivism is based on pragmatism. The philosophers William James and John Dewey are the major theorists in this pedagogical paradigm. The curriculum was built on real world problem solving and is experience-centered as well as student-centered.

Postmodernism is grounded in existentialism. Henry Giroux and Paulo Freire are the thinkers in this area. According to the postmodernists the establishment controls the curriculum so the key to education is the study of underrepresented groups. These thinkers would teach ideas outside the scope of the curriculum standards.

Social reconstructionists believed that schools could reconstruct society. Harold Rugg, George Counts, and Theodore Brameld are the major advocates of this approach. Social reconstructionists are sometimes called radical progressives. They attempt to change the world by having students do service learning activities to make life better.

Discussion Questions

1. What is history? Define it and explain the cyclical nature of it? Does history have a use value to society?
2. What impact did Charles Darwin have on intellectual history?
3. What is philosophy? Does it have a use value to society?
4. What are the fields of philosophy?
5. What are the traditional philosophies?
6. What are the modern theories of education?

References & Further Reading

Aristotle. (1994) *The complete works of aristotle*. Oxford: Clarendon Press.

Augustine. (1909) *Confessions*. New York: P.F. Collier & Son.

Cubberley, E.P. (1948) *History of education: educational practice and process considered a phase of the development of western civilization*. New York: Houghton Mifflin

Dewey, J. (1989) *Art as experience*. Edwardsville: Southern Illinois University Press.

Gutek, G.L. (1997) *Philosophical and ideological perspectives on education*. Boston: Allyn and Bacon.

Hegel, G.W.RF. (1895) *Lectures on the philosophy of religion*. London: Kegan Paul, Trench, Trubner.

Kierkegaard, S. (1983) *Fear and trembling*. Princeton: Princeton University Press.

Kuhn, T. (1962) *The structure of scientific revolutions*. Chicago: University of Chicago Press.

McKay, J. P., B.D. Hill & J. Buckler (1999) *A history of western society*. New York: Houghton Mifflin.

Power, E. J. (1991) *A legacy of learning: A history of western civilization*. Albany: State University of New York Press.

Plato. (1888) *Republic*. Oxford: Clarendon Press

Walford, E. (1877) *The politics and economics of aristotle*. London: Bell & Dalby

Whitehead, A.N. (1929) *The aims of education*. New York: New American Library

Wittgenstein, L. (1958) *The blue and brown books*. New York: Harper & Row.

Chapter 2
The Cradles of Western Education and the Beginnings of Literacy

Explain the significance of:

People: Sumerians, Egyptians, Hebrews, Vienna School of Ethnology

Terms: periods of early culture, Neolithic revolution, Bronze Age, Iron Age, ethical monotheism, cuneiform, hieroglyphics, transhumance, scribes

Pre-Literate Societies

The earliest eras known to history were the periods of early culture referred to as the Stone, Bronze, and Iron Ages. The modern day Middle East is where these cultures developed. These epochs were named for the primary substance used in making weapons and tools.

The Stone Age

The Stone Age was divided by social scientists into three parts the Old, Middle, and New Stone Ages. During the Old Stone Age (c.500,000-10,000 BC) people were hunters and food gathers. They were nomadic with no permanent settlement because they had to move around in order to find food. Their chief occupation was the struggle to survive. Education was learning to hunt animals and gather plants to eat. Instruction was in the form of imitation of the adult activities for meeting the basic needs of food, shelter and clothing.

The Middle Stone Age (c. 10,000 BC - 5,000 BC) was a transitional stage between transhumance (hunting and food gathering) and living in settlements. At this time, people began to live in villages, farm, and domesticate animals.

According to the Vienna School of Ethnology, a prominent anthropological-historical theory, grains were first cultivated in the Middle East and animals were first domesticated in Northern Europe. During the Middle Stone Age education took place at home and children imitated adults in hunting, food gathering, and building shelters.

The New Stone Age (c. 8,000 BC -2,500 BC) is sometimes called "the Neolithic revolution." During this time-frame, people developed many advanced characteristics of civilization such as the widespread domestication of animals. The beginnings of scientific agriculture and the ceramic arts also appeared during this era. Elders taught children hunting, food gathering, growing crops, making pottery, and building shelters.

The Bronze Age

The next major era was the Bronze Age (c 3,000 BC – 1,000 BC). During this time, cities developed as well as commercial contacts with other peoples and cultures. The beginnings of literacy occurred at this time. Writing was needed to develop fair contracts, so scribes, or people who could write, were important. For this reason, scribes were given a formal education.

The Iron Age

The last of the three periods of early culture was the Iron Age (c. 1,000 BC) and this was the period of written documents. Due to the need for governmental and economic records, literacy dominated the functions of many groups of people. Thus the epoch of written records began.

Early Antiquity and Literacy

Mesopotamia

According to archeologists, the earliest writing began in Mesopotamia between 3,400 BC and 3,200 BC. The first writing was pictographic and was limited to certain ideas. Certain pictures meant things. For example, a star meant guidance, an eye depicted seeing, and the sun was the symbol for warmth. Later, writing took the form of a pictograph and it expressed an ideograph in which the picture was phonetically pronounced and became a phonogram, such as a picture of a bee and a leaf became belief.

The Sumerians developed the art of writing around 3,500 BC. These people wrote the first literature, *The Epic of Gilgamesh*, which included a story about a man who built an ark and a great flood. They also had the first written laws, *Hammurabi's Law Code*. With its focus on writing and literacy, the most important persons in Sumerian society were the scribes. Kings established schools for teaching the scribes the craft of writing. The Sumerians wrote on clay tablets with a stylus using wedged shaped characters called cuneiform.

The Egyptians and the Hebrews

The Egyptians wrote on papyrus and their writings were called hieroglyphics. These people had a high level of culture and education. They taught physicians, architects, linguists, and diplomats.

The Hebrews developed a high level of theological understanding that advocated ethical monotheism. Ethical monotheism was the idea of one god that not only demanded ritual, but also correct or ethical behavior.

Discussion Questions

1. Discuss the characteristics of the period of early culture.
2. What was cuneiform? What were hieroglyphics?
3. What were the contributions of the Egyptians and the Hebrews?

References & Further Reading

Cantor, N.F. (2004) *Antiquity: From the birth of sumerian civilization to the fall of rome*. New York: Harper

Cubberley, E.P. (1948) *History of education: Educational practice and process considered a phase of the development of western civilization*. New York: Houghton Mifflin

MacKendrick, P., D. J. Genakoplos, J.H. Hexter, & R. Pipes.(1968) *Western civilization*. New York: Harper and Row

McKay, J. P., B.D. Hill & J. Buckler (1999) *A history of western society*. New York: Houghton Mifflin.

Chapter 3
The Greeks

Explain the significance of:

People: King Minos, Homer, King Darius, King Xerxes, Pericles, Aeschylus, Sophocles, Socrates, Plato, Aristotle, Alexander the Great, Aristippus

Terms: bull leaping, Minoans, Mycenaean culture, *The Illiad and Odyssey*, Dorans, first Persian war, marathon run, Peloponnesian Wars, *Oedipus Rex*, Laconia, *piadomonos*, "Come back with your shield or on it!", *ephors*, "A night and a day!", spartan environment, Attica, Council of 500, Assembly of Citizens, census of 44BC, "A sound mind in a sound body!", *pedagogue, paedotribe, grammatist, citharist*, sophists, "The Socratic method". idealism, *Dialogues, The Republic*, philosopher-king, "Allegory of the Cave", realism, hellenistic age, "To the strongest!", *ephebic* schools, age-graded schools

Early History

Greek civilization began on the island of Crete. This culture was called Minoan after their King Minos. Minos built a great palace at Knossos. The Minoans had an advanced society. For example, their houses had an ingenious heating and cooling system that was fueled by running water through the walls. They also had a spectator sport, bull leaping. This sport was the forerunner to both gymnastics and bull fighting.

Around 1100 BC, the Minoans left Crete and migrated to the Greek mainland. Historians have no idea why they migrated. Interestingly, some scholars theorize a great catastrophe such as an earthquake or a tidal wave occurred, causing the migration.

The civilization the early Greeks built on the mainland was called the Mycenaean culture. The Mycenaeans made war on Troy. The Greeks won the Trojan War by the use of a so-called "Trojan horse." This was the first evidence of
camouflage being used in war. The Greeks built a giant wooden horse and
placed it in front of the Trojan gate. The people of the metropolis thought the
horse was a peace offering and they brought it into the city. When night fell, the
Greeks, who were hiding in the horse, got out of it, and destroyed the Trojans.
Much of what we know of the Trojan War comes from the Greek writer, Homer.

Homeric Education

Homer's books, The *Iliad* and the *Odyssey,* were epic works that relate the
Greek struggle with Troy. These stories constituted a movement from oral to
written traditions based on universal philosophical themes. Homeric education
transmitted Greek culture. It gave the Greeks a cultural identity as well as
examples of character and morality. In essence, these epics acculturated the
Greek youth. The *Iliad* was an account of the cause, course, and outcome of the
Trojan War. The *Odyssey* was an account of the Greeks' thirty year journey
back to Mycenae. Both of these books contained moral lessons for the Greeks.
They were a fatalistic people who believed that the evil one does comes back
to haunt him or her, as the good that one does ennobles him or her.

War and Migration

The Dorans invaded the Greek mainland. This caused a massive Greek migration to Asia Minor. In Asia Minor, the Greeks built cities and developed colonies. These colonies brought wealth, and put the Greeks into direct conflict
with the Persians. A new rich middle class developed in Asia Minor, which
caused concern for the Persians. This apprehension led to hostilities.

The Persians saw the Greek colonies as an economic and political threat, so
they made war on the Greeks. King Darius led the first Persian war in 490 BC.
The Athenians defeated the Persians at the Battle of Marathon, after which the
invaders withdrew from the peninsula. The Greeks sent a messenger back to
Athens who ran 26 miles to Athens and died upon his arrival. Marathon runs
today honor that event. Darius' son, King Xerxes, returned to Greece in 480 BC
to initiate the second Persian war. Xerxes' fleet was destroyed by the Greeks at
the Battle of Salamis. During the battle, an Athenian princess in command of the
Greek fleet rammed Xerxes' ship. Upon seeing this, Xerxes withdrew from the
peninsula never to return.

No longer having an external threat, the Greeks made war on each other in
the Peloponnesian wars. The major combatants were the city-states of Athens
and Sparta. During the conflict, Pericles emerged as a great democratic leader
for the Athenians. At the end of the first year of war, he gave a powerful speech
before the Athenian dead. In this speech, which has been compared to Lincoln's
Gettysburg Address and John F. Kennedy's Inaugural Address, Pericles extolled

the virtues of democracy. The war so weakened the Greeks that the Macedo-
nians under King Philip came down from the north to conquer them, thereby,
ending the era of Greek dominance.

Greek Cultural Patterns

The Greeks had a male-dominated, slaveholding society. This society
created some of the most enduring stories in world literature. Greek drama consisted of comedies and tragedies. The most famous of the playwrights were Aeschylus, Sophocles, and Euripides. The most notable Greek play was *Oedipus
Rex*. This was a tragedy about a man who unknowingly killed his father and
married his mother. Supposedly, during the 1930s, Sigmund Freud, the great
Viennese psychoanalyst, developed his "Oedipus complex" while watching the
play.

Cultural and political aspects of Greek life centered on the "city-state" or
"polis." The word "political" or "politics" is derived from "polis." The political
development of the polis involved several different types of government. The
paradigms that evolved were: monarchy (rule of a king), aristocracy (rule of the
upper class), plutocracy (rule of the rich), oligarchy (rule of a few), democracy
(rule of the people), and tyranny (rule of a tyrant). Today we generally think of
tyrants as bad. However, in ancient times, tyrants ruled in emergencies then
gave back power after the emergency was over.

Sparta and Athens

Two city-states dominated the Greek peninsula, Sparta and Athens. Sparta
was a military oligarchy and Athens was a pure democracy.

The Polis of Laconia

The polis of Laconia had the city of Sparta as its capital. Sparta was a fas-
cistic state dedicated to war and its own preservation as a political entity. Education was practical and military. A Spartan official called a *piadomonos* super-
vised Laconian education. This schooling was harsh and often cruel. Girls, from
an early age, were taught domestic skills at home. Boys, at the age of 7, were
raised as soldiers and lived in barracks. They were trained in all forms of military science and were starved. To eat, they were given only a thin black soup of
whatever vegetable or grain was available. The boys were encouraged to steal in
order to survive under combat conditions. However, if they were caught steal-
ing, they would be flogged. In order to graduate, a Spartan boy had to kill a
slave with his bare hands and not get caught.

Before a battle, the soldier's mother, girlfriend, or wife would say: "Come
back with your shield or on it!" The Spartans had very heavy shields. If they
came back with the shield they were victorious. If they came back on it, they
were wounded or had died in battle. Loved ones assumed they lost but fought

bravely. If they came back without the shield, it would signify they deserted battle and were a disgrace.

Laconians were also cruel to the weak. If a child was born weak and sickly it was brought before the executive council of five *ephors* who would determine the baby's fate. "A night and a day!" would be uttered by the *ephors*. This phrase meant that the child must spend a day and night exposed to the elements on a hillside. If the infant survived, it was strong enough to be a Spartan. If it died, it wasn't tough enough to be a Spartan. Today the term, "Spartan environment" is used to mean a harsh climate or treatment. The term is justly warranted.

The Polis of Attica

The polis of Attica had its capital at Athens. Athens developed a humane, rational and individualistic culture based on philosophical premises of reason, truth, and justice. The Athenian city-state was a pure democracy in that every citizen had a say in governmental policy. The government consisted of an Assembly of Citizens who voted on measures and a Council of 500 who executed these measures. The census of 44 BC revealed that out of a population of 140,000, only 40,000 citizens exercised their liberties. Education in Athens can be summed up in their credo: "A sound mind in a sound body!" To carry out this particular curricular manifestation, Athenians had many teachers with various roles. A *pedagogue* was a tutor, a *paedotribe* was a physical education instructor, a *grammatist* was a teacher of reading, and a *citharist* taught music

Greek Educational Paradigms

The Greeks developed the first coherent systems of philosophy in the city-state of Athens. The first of these thinkers were collectively known as the Sophists. The Sophists were itinerant teachers of rhetoric who claimed to be able to teach anyone anything. They instructed their pupils on how to be good legislators and consumers of information. This, of course, was necessary in the Athenian pure democracy where every citizen was technically a member of the legislature. The Sophists taught communication skills to develop advocates who could persuade, motivate, and accept a point of view. Not everyone liked the Sophists because they charged tuition. They were actually the first teachers to do so. Others disliked them because their ideas were tentative and there was no ultimate moral guide in their philosophy.

The Philosophical Greats

Socrates

Socrates developed a simple system of ethics based on a life of moral excellence and an idea that truth existed within everyone. The teacher had to bring that truth out in each pupil by means of questioning. This questioning technique became know as "the Socratic method." This method consisted of answering a question with another question and leading the student to knowledge. This method is currently used in law schools. Socrates believed that education liberated students to discover new ideas.

Socrates developed universal principles of goodness, beauty, and truth that governed human conduct. Socrates was a gadfly on the body politic of Attica. As a result, he got out of political favor when his friends lost power and his enemies came after him. Socrates was made to drink poison hemlock for corrupting the youth of Athens and not worshipping the gods. Much of what we know of Socrates comes from his student Plato.

Plato

Plato was Socrates' disciple for many years. In a series of *Dialogues*, Plato related the philosophy of Socrates. Many historians believe that Plato put words in Socrates' mouth to favor his own ideas. Plato formulated the philosophy of idealism. This philosophy is concerned with the realm of ideas. Plato believed that the only true reality was mathematics because every time he worked out an equation he got the same answer. He hypothesized that since truth is in numbers it must also be in nature and society. The problem was to find it. For Plato, reality was the unchanging world of perfect ideas and imperfect representations in the world.

Plato elaborated on these concepts in his book about the perfect society that he titled *The Republic*. In this utopia, there were three classes of society. The philosopher-kings were rulers who had to study philosophy for 42 years. This gave them insights into reality that ordinary people did not have, thus they had the right to govern. The second class of people was the guardians and they were warriors and protectors. The guardians held everything in common including families. The lowest caste of people was the workers who labored on mundane tasks for the good of society.

Plato's conception of metaphysics can be explained by the "Allegory of the Cave." In the allegory, most people sit in a cave and are chained by ignorance to look at the reflection of reality through the shadows of a fire. Only the philosopher-king can see true reality because he turns around and looks outside seeing reality as it is. In essence, what Plato did was to intellectualize his metaphysics by suggesting that reality and truth reside in the mind and not in the real world of observation.

Aristotle

Aristotle, one of Plato's pupils, disagreed with his mentor and believed that reality and truth reside in the real world and not in the mind. Therefore, Aristotle formulated the philosophy known as realism. Realists believe in rationalism, observation, and natural laws as they are mechanisms for determining reality. Aristotle believed in scientific observation. Plato thought that reality was intellectual, whereas Aristotle believed it was technical. Aristotle became the tutor of Alexander the Great, and he instilled in Alexander a deep respect and love of learning. As a result, Alexander took scribes wherever he went to record what they saw and the deeds they had done for future generations.

All of these thinkers were teachers and philosophers, but Isocrates, the great Athenian teacher of rhetoric, was a thinker and philosopher of teaching. Isocrates taught rhetorical knowledge for civic reform and rational expression of thought. He was concerned with the best method of instruction to instill these ideas in others.

The Greeks have left a lasting legacy of intellectual thought and debate. Their philosophies can be summed up in the concept of self which was ahead of its time. The individual becomes important to Western society. As Aristotle said, "Wonders never cease, and man is most wonderful."

Hellenistic Education

The Hellenistic Age was the period of time from the death of Alexander the Great to the rise of Rome. It was a blending of Greek and Roman culture. After the Peloponnesian Wars, Philip of Macedon conquered the Greeks. Macedon was a land to the north of the Greek Peninsula. After the conquest, Philip was murdered and his son, Alexander, unified the Greeks by giving them a common enemy in the Persians. He made war on Persia and conquered the greatest empire the world had ever seen. In Babylon, Alexander drank bad wine and died. On his deathbed he was asked to whom did he leave his empire. His answer was: "To the strongest," because he knew that his generals would fight over his holdings and none would be greater than he.

Alexander's conquests became the framework for Hellenistic civilization. It was his vision, as taught to him by Aristotle, that a fusion of all the best things from Greek and Persian society would lead to a lasting peace if cultural differences did not cloud the issue. Therefore, the period ushered in by Alexander's conquests, the Hellenistic Age, gave the world its first multicultural society.

Hellenistic education was influenced by Aristippus' book: *On Education*. In this work, Aristippus advocated a curriculum rich in classical literature, involving the reading and analysis of ancient texts. *On Education* dominated the pedagogy of the Hellenistic Age.

In the Hellenistic period, the schools were state-controlled and age-graded. Age-graded schools were institutions in which students of the same age were taught together, which is a common practice today, but not in the ancient world. Sports in the schools declined, but sports clubs flourished.

Both boys and girls attended the primary, elementary, and secondary schools. Primary education was done in the home and involved children to the age of six. They were taught manners and morals. At the age of seven, students attended elementary schools, and were taught by professional teachers in a holistic fashion. The curriculum included literacy, reading, writing, counting, drawing, dancing, and music. Students remained in the elementary schools until the age of fourteen. At that age, they attended secondary schools where they learned literature, science, grammar, geometry, astronomy, music, and math. Male students attended *ephebic* schools between the ages of eighteen and twenty. These institutions dealt essentially with military matters. These schools were publicly supported, but higher education was not state-funded.

The students who continued their education past the age of 20 had to pay tuition. Medical schools, schools of rhetoric, schools of philosophy, and museums were the major educational institutions at this level. Museums were actually ancient think tanks where kings and queens would have scholars do applied and pure research for various reasons.

The legacy of Hellenistic education is the age-graded school with a multicultural perspective on students. The curriculum was a precursor to the medieval concept of the Seven Liberal Arts. The Hellenistic period serves as an historical bridge between the classical civilizations Greece and Rome.

Discussion Questions

1. What were the Minoan civilization and the Myceanaean civilization?
2. Explain Homeric education.
3. What were the Persian Wars and the Peloponnesian Wars?
4. What was the Greek "polis"?
5. Compare and contrast the city-states of Sparta and Athens.
6. Analyze the Athenian census of 44BC and evaluate Athenian democracy.
7. Explain Plato's "Allegory of the Cave".
8. Compare and contrast the philosophies of Socrates, Plato and Aristotle.
9. Discuss the achievements of the Hellenistic Age.

References & Further Reading

Aristotle. (1994) *The complete works of aristotle*. Oxford: Clarendon Press.

Cantor, N.F. (2004) *Antiquity: From the birth of sumerian civilization to the fall of rome*. New York: Harper

Chambliss, J.J. (1971*) Nobility, tragedy, and naturalism: Education in ancient greece*. Minneapolis; Burgess.

Cubberley, E.P. (1948) *History of education: Educational practice and process considered a phase of the development of western civilization*. New York: Houghton Mifflin

MacKendrick, P., D. J. Genakoplos, J.H. Hexter, & R. Pipes. (1968) *Western civilization*. New York: Harper and Row

McKay, J. P., B.D. Hill & J. Buckler (1999) *A history of western society*. New York: Houghton Mifflin.

Plato. (1888) *Republic*. Oxford: Clarendon Press

Walford, E. (1877) *The politics and economics of aristotle*. London: Bell & Dalby

Chapter 4
The Romans

Explain the significance of:

People: Romulus and Remus, Tarquin the Proud, Julius Caesar, Brutus, Octavius, Marc Antony, Cicero, Quintilian, Seneca, Plutarch, Diocletian, Justinian, M. Rostovteff

Terms: Roman founding myth, *SPQR*, Tribunes, Punic Wars, Plebeian, Patrician, *ludi* magister, pedagogue, *rhetor*, professor, *Pax Romano*, *Codex Justinus*

Early History

In its early development Rome was isolated due to geography. The Italian Peninsula and the Alps to the north gave the Latin tribes autonomy in the early stages of this civilization's cultural development. The most advanced of the Latin tribes were the Etruscans, who built and dominated the area for centuries.

Rome was founded in myth when two brothers, Romulus and Remus, fought each other for control of their tribe. The myth relates that a she-wolf raised them and they grew into strong men. The fight lasted for several days when Romulus finally defeated Remus. The spot of his victory was a valley with seven hills, and there Romulus built the city of Rome. Etruscan kings dominated the Romans until the reign of Tarquin the Proud. In 510 BC, the Romans overthrew Tarquin and set up a republican form of government.

The basis for the Roman government was the Twelve Tablets. These laws, inscribed on twelve tablets, gave equality under the law to both Plebeians or lower class Romans, and Patricians or upper class Romans. The Romans were so proud of their government that they put SPQR on their banners, which meant *Senatus Populusque Romanus* (The Senate and People of Rome). The government under the Republic had two officials, usually generals, who were "Tribunes of the People." As Tribunes, they had the right to "veto" or "say no" to any measure passed that would hurt the poor people. The republic flourished until the Punic Wars, coming from the Latin *Punis*, meaning Phoenician. The wars were between Rome and Carthage for control of the Mediterranean trade routes. These military campaigns extended Roman power and made it a complex state. The Romans, essentially, had a government for a city now governing an empire. Thus, the republic began to decay in favor of dictator generals such as Sulla, and Caesar who could deal with the difficulties of a world power.

On March 15 in 44 BC, Julius Caesar was assassinated on the floor of the Roman Senate. Caesar was a dictator and the Romans were suspect of one-man rule. The conspirators were more of his friends than his enemies. Even his adopted son, Brutus stabbed him. Supposedly, Caesar's last words were: "*Et tu, Brute?*" meaning in Latin, "You too Brutus?" As soon as Caesar was dead, his generals began to fight over his empire. The major combatants were Marc Antony and Octavius, another of Caesar's adopted sons. At the Battle of Actium, Octavius defeated Antony and gained dictatorial control of Rome, thereby, setting up a new government called the *Principate*. This government was simply a façade of Republicanism from below and total control by the *Princeps* or first citizen from the top. Octavian, who changed his name to Augustus, became Rome's first emperor.

Roman Education

Roman education was greatly influenced by the Greeks, especially the Hellenistic educational paradigm. Boys between the ages of six or seven until eighteen attended the *ludi*, or primary school, in which the *ludi magister* was the instructor. At this institution the students were taught reading, writing, and reckoning (counting). Upper class students had a *pedagogue*, or Greek slave, as a tutor. A *grammaticus* taught students between the ages of twelve and sixteen grammar and literature in Latin grammar schools. Between the ages of sixteen and nineteen, students would study grammar, rhetoric, dialectics, and law with a *rhetor* at collegiate schools of rhetoric. Students who continued their education beyond the age of 20 were taught by *professors* who taught law, medicine, architecture, mathematics, grammar, and rhetoric at the University of Rome or the Greek universities. These schools evolved over a period of time and they all flourished under the *Pax Romano*, the 200 year Roman peace beginning with the reign of Augustus.

Roman Educators

Cicero

Cicero was a great orator in Rome. He taught oratory as a prerequisite for citizenship. He was one of the first to see the advantages of oratory and citizen participation. He wrote *de Oratoria*. He integrated both Greek and Roman conceptions of speaking. Cicero believed in a classic study that included the liberal arts, oratory, and jurisprudence. He reasoned that if all citizens could argue like lawyers, the Republic could sustain itself through any tribulation. Therefore, Cicero's curriculum consisted of rational argument for the public good through a jurisprudence approach.

Quintilian

Quintilian was a progressive educator in Rome. He was so successful the emperor named him the chief educator of the empire. He believed that learning must be appropriate to the pupil's abilities and readiness. According to Quintilian, there were two stages of developmental learning. The first stage was the sensory experience stage, from ages seven to fourteen, in which ideas, memory, and literature were stressed in an experiential environment. The second stage was the reasoning stage, from ages fourteen to seventeen, in which the liberal arts and grammar were taught. Quintilian was the first teacher of Latin rhetoric in Rome. His ideas were leaning toward Christianity. He believed that socialization was an important process in education.

Quintilian wrote down his educational philosophy in his book, *Institutio Oratoria*. In that work, he stated in that education should be based on the stages of development from childhood to adulthood. He devised specific lessons suited to pupils' readiness and ability to learn. This was the first coherent attempt at sequential learning theory applied to instruction. He also believed that teachers should motivate their students by making learning more attractive and interesting.

Seneca and Plutarch

Seneca was the tutor of Nero. Nero was one of the demented emperors of Rome, who supposedly played the fiddle while Rome burned. Seneca attempted to teach him about natural law and individual freedom, but Nero did not learn and instead created a legacy of death and destruction during his reign.

Plutarch was a moralist who stressed tradition, reason, and habit. He taught history through biography and is remembered for his book *Parallel Lives of Famous Greeks and Romans*. The Stoics, Plato and Aristotle, influenced him. He believed in the preservation of traditional values tested through experience and learning by biographical example.

The Division of the Empire

Prior to the fall of Rome, the emperor Diocletian separated the empire into two separate administrative units: The Western Roman Empire and the Eastern Roman Empire. Later, Constantine moved the capital from Rome in the West to Byzantium in the East, and renamed the capital Constantinople. The Western Empire was overrun by the Germanic tribes and officially fell in 476 AD.

The Roman Empire in the East became known as the Byzantine Empire and survived for another 1000 years until 1453 AD. In addition, it preserved Greco-Roman Civilization until the High Middle Ages and the Renaissance enabled European scholars to relearn the Classics. The greatest of the Byzantine emperors was Justinian. He was the preserver of Roman law. He commissioned the *Codex Justinus* which was three books of Roman law consisting of legislative law, judicial law, and Justinian-made law. These books were the foundational works that would later inspire graduate schools of law at great European universities like Cambridge, Oxford, and Paris.

Decline and Fall

According to the Russian historian, M. Rostovteff, the Roman decline was caused by a collective barbarism which made it fashionable to be ignorant. Other historians have postulated many reasons for the decline and fall of the Roman state, law, and society. These reasons included political over-extension, manpower shortages, irresponsibility of the elite, and military absolutism. Despite its fall, Rome made many contributions to educational history in theory, philosophy, and practice.

Discussion Questions

1. Discuss the mythical founding of Rome.
2. Explain "SPQR".
3. Who were Julius Caesar and Octavian?
4. List the various schools and the name of the teachers' titles in the Roman schools.
5. Explain the educational theories of:
   a. Cicero
   b. Quintilian
   c. Seneca
   d. Plutarch
6. Why was the Roman Empire divided?
7. Does the Rostovteff thesis adequately explain Rome's decline and fall?
8. What was the contribution of Justinian to Western education?

References & Further Reading

Cantor, N.F. (2004) *Antiquity: From the birth of sumerian civilization to the fall of rome.* New York: Harper

Chambliss, J.J. (1971) *Nobility, tragedy, and naturalism: Education in ancient greece.* Minneapolis: Burgess.

Cubberley, E.P. (1948) History of education: Educational practice and process considered a phase of the development of western civilization. New York: Houghton Mifflin.

MacKendrick, P., D. J. Genakoplos, J.H. Hexter, & R. Pipes. (1968) *Western civilization.* New York: Harper and Row

Power, E. J. (1991) *A legacy of learning: A history of western civilization.* Albany: State University of New York Press

Quintilian. (1905) *The institutes of oratory.* London: Dewick & Clark.

Chapter 5
The Medievalists & Scholasticism

Explain the significance of:

People: Charles Martel, Clovis, Pepin the Short, Charlemagne, Alcuin, Voltaire, Pope Gregory VII, Henry IV, Alexis Comenius, Pope Urban II, Louis the Pious, Berrenger, Lanfranc, Averrores, St. Thomas Aquinas, William of Ockham, Francisco Petrarch, Albertus Magnus

Terms: Middle Ages, medieval world view, feudalism, manorialism, homage, fealty, benefice or *feudus*, tripartite system, subinfeudation, medieval pyramid, Franks, Battle of Tours, December 25, 800 AD, *Dialogue Textbook*, Holy Roman Empire, petrine supremacy, caesaro-papism, lay investiture, crusades, *trivium*, *quadvium*, seven liberal arts, craft education, chivalric education, student guild, *disputatio*, theology, *lectura*, degrees, schoolmen, faith to reason, scholasticism, *Summa Theologia*, prime mover

Historical Overview

The medieval period, or the Middle Ages, was considered to be the epoch between the fall of Rome 476 AD to the 15th Century. The 15th Century is considered "modern times," so the "Middle Ages" are between ancient and modern times. The first 500 years of the medieval age are known as the "Dark Ages" roughly from 500 to 1000 AD. The second 500 years of the medieval age are known as the "High Middle Ages" roughly from 1000 to 1500 AD. At this time, Western Christianity dominated the medieval worldview. Christian doctrine, Roman legalism, a hierarchical system, and sacred scriptures were the major elements of epistemological understanding during this time. Doctrinal instruction and the sacramental system governed educational beliefs. The purpose of education was religious and involved teaching clergy and adherents. This caused a dualism in medieval thought processes symbolized by the monastery and the tavern. The monastery was symbolic of the here-after and the tavern was symbolic of the here and now.

This dualism caused Western society at this time to seem somewhat disjointed and decentralized. The Pope, who became the most powerful person in Europe took up the power void left by the decline of Roman political state. Adding to this confusion was the paradigm of feudalism, the system of mutual protection brought about by the fall of Rome. No centralized authority existed in Europe, except the Pope in Rome. Manoralism was the economic basis of feudalism with all economic activity for the region occurring around the manor house.

The Feudal Contract and Subinfeudation

Feudalism was based on the feudal contract and the tripartite system. The feudal contract had several parts. The first part was known as the homage. This was where the lesser lord swore an allegiance to a greater lord. The second part was known as the fealty. In fealty, the greater lord and the lesser lord swore allegiance to each other. The third part was known as the benefice or *feudus*. In *feudus*, the greater lord gave the lesser lord a fief or piece of land in exchange for protection. Today, the contract is a basic rudiment of Western law.

The tripartite system also supported the feudal society. This was a hierarchical system based on three distinct classes of people who had a pronounced role in the process of mutual protection: lords, knights, and serfs. The lords ruled the manor. The knights fought and protected the lords and serfs. The serfs worked the land in exchange for shelter and protection.

The feudal system worked well until a problem known as subinfeudation occurred as a result of the complex web of alliances brought about by the feudal system. Subinfeudation developed when a greater lord made a vassal of a lesser lord who had allegiance to more than one greater lord. The commitment to more than one person caused confusion of allegiance and blurred the feudal system's protective features.

The Medieval Pyramid

A strict hierarchy of society replaced the designation of central authority at this time. This culture was dualistic and had a temporal and spiritual side. However, in both paradigms, God was at the top of the pyramid. The temporal ladder started after God with the king then proceeded to greater and lesser nobility, freedmen, and lastly serfs. The spiritual ladder started after God with the Pope then proceeded to cardinals and bishops, priests and nuns, and lastly brothers.

This hierarchy was rigid and adhered to without question during the Early Middle Ages.

The Early Middle Ages and The Carolingian Renaissance

A Germanic tribe, the Franks, came to dominate Europe. Frankish rule began with Charles Martel, "The Hammer," who in 776 AD defeated the Moors at the Battle of Tours. The ancestors of Martel became the kings of the Franks. Later, Clovis, a descendent of Martel, had a Christian wife who urged him to convert to Christianity. Supposedly, during battle, Clovis saw a vision of a cross in the sky and converted to Christianity. This conversion made the Franks the only Christian Germanic tribe. Pepin the Short, another Frankish king, had to constantly fight for the Pope. Therefore, the Franks had a very close relationship to the Papacy. A great ruler of the Franks became king. He was the grandson of Pepin and was called Charles the Great, more commonly referred to as Charlemagne. During his reign he created what has been called the Carolingian Renaissance.

Charlemagne hired the scholar, Alciun of York, and together they set up the educational system in Europe. Alciun, at the behest of Charles, built a palace school at Aachen, the capital of the Frankish Kingdom. At that institution, Alciun developed the first modern textbooks called *Dialogue Textbooks* because they were in a question and answer format like a catechism. Later, the king decreed that schools be built throughout his kingdom. Charlemagne was a great educational reformer but he was also a warrior, and he fought battles to convert the pagan Germanic tribes to Christianity. This caused him to convert by the sword as evidenced in his massacre of Saxon nobles at Verdun in 782 AD.

On December 25, 800 AD, the Pope crowned Charlemagne Holy Roman Emperor. He called his empire *Magna Germania* or Greater Germany but the Pope renamed it the Holy Roman Empire. The Holy Father believed that it would have the glory of old Rome and be sanctified by Christianity. The French historian Voltaire analyzed *Magna Germania* and stated that: "The Holy Roman Empire was neither holy, nor Roman, nor an empire!" This statement was very true in that the empire wasn't holy because many were not Christian, it wasn't Roman because it was mainly German, and it wasn't an empire because it was more like a loose confederation.

The Seven Liberal Arts

The curriculum developed by Alciun was called the *studium generale*. The core curriculum was known as the *trivium* and consisted of grammar, rhetoric, and logic or dialectics. Grammar was the art of writing well, rhetoric was the art of speaking well, and logic or dialectics was the art of reasoning well or using logic to win arguments of a metaphysical nature. The advanced curriculum was called the *quadvium* and consisted of arithmetic, geometry, astronomy, and music. Music was a series of nine subjects guarded by the nine muses. The most important of these muses was Clio the muse of history. Collectively, these subjects became know as the "Seven Liberal Arts". After the reign of Charlemagne, the Seven Liberal Arts were lost to Europe but preserved by Irish monks who saved them for Western civilization. The Seven Liberal Arts became the basis of Western education during the High Middle Ages and the Renaissance.

Petrine Supremacy versus Caesaro-Papism and the Crusades

After the reign of Charlemagne, Europe fell into chaos as the feudal system took hold of temporal society and the Pope became the most powerful man in Europe as both worldly and spiritual power were his. This led to a conflict between monarchs and Popes known as petrine supremacy versus caesaro-papism. Petrine supremacy was the belief that the Pope was supreme in all matters and caesaro-papism was the belief that the monarch within his or her state was supreme in all matters. This problem reached its zenith during the argument between Pope Gregory VII and King Henry IV of Germany. Lay investiture was a practice of monarchs appointing bishops. Pope Gregory forbade this and Henry invested bishops anyway. The conflict reached a climax when Gregory excommunicated Henry and Henry had to beg the Pope to forgive him by praying for three days in a snowdrift wearing a sackcloth. It appeared as if petrine supremacy had won out over caesaro-papism.

The next great exercise in Papal dominance was the crusades. The Byzantine emperor, Alexius Comenius wrote a letter to Pope Urban II asking for his help against the Islamics from Arabia. Urban made Comenius' cause his own and at Clermont he gave a speech that started the crusading movement. The speech at Clermont was a fiery oration, which caused the armies of Europe to attempt to regain the Holy Land from the Islamic Turks. In a larger sense, it was also an effort to spread Christianity by the sword as Charlemagne did during his reign over *Magna Germania*. Some scholars see the crusades, particularly the ones conducted by Louis the Pious, as the noblest idealism of Western man, while others consider them an example of barbarism.

Chivalric and Craft Education

Due to the crusades, many changes occurred in Europe. Nobles gave charters to towns in exchange for money. The charter freed the inhabitants of the towns from the feudal obligation, enabling them to pursue careers other than "boonwork" for the lord of the manor. Therefore, many chose crafts as a career option. Craft education consisted of three stages: apprentice, journeyman, and master craftsman. At the age of seven, the child would be taught the trade from a master craftsman as an apprentice. At the age of fourteen, the novice would go around making his wares and selling them to people as a journeyman. Lastly, the neophyte would produce a masterpiece in his trade and it would be judged by his respective guild whereupon he would become a master craftsman. Today, many occupations such as pipefitting, and coopering or barrel making must go through similar learning stages as the medieval craftsman.

Chivalric education was also modeled on the multiples of seven system because of the seven sacraments. A boy became a page at the age of seven and he learned manners and morals from the lady of the manor. He also was taught to play the knightly game of chess. At fourteen, the boy became a squire and was basically an apprentice to a knight. He would learn horsemanship and fighting on horseback. When he was twenty-one years of age, he had to find a sponsor to buy his armor and golden spurs that were all very expensive. After a twenty-four hour prayer vigil, he would go through the accolade or ceremony of knighting. Lastly, he would have to jump on his horse in full armor without touching the stirrups to become a knight.

We find, in current educational practice, internships in all fields of study that are the legacy of both the medieval craft and chivalric educational systems. The concept of "learning by doing," first applied to medieval craftsmanship and knighthood training, is now the mainstay of most modern pedagogical paradigms. Furthermore, this heritage of learning can be seen in the development of the university and scholarship as seen in the scholastic movement of the period.

The Medieval University and Scholasticism

The medieval university began as a student guild. The purpose of the organization was to set up lectures as well as hire and fire the professors. In the beginning, these institutions were run by the students. Over the years, various layers of bureaucracy have left the universities today out of the control of either students or professors but instead in the hands of educated and uneducated administrators which puts an extra layer of bureaucracy between the students and their instructors.

The historical roots of the medieval university began with the Carolingian Renaissance around 800 AD. This was the time of Charlemagne and Alcuin of York who, together, developed the Seven Liberal Arts. After Charles the Great's rule, Irish monks continued to write, discuss and teach the Seven Liberal Arts during the Dark Ages. The monks preserved them for Western society. During the High Middle Ages, the Seven Liberal Arts became the major curricula of the all institutions of higher learning in the West.

Teaching Methods, Faculties, and Degrees

The methods of instruction in the university consisted of two techniques: the *lectura*, or lecture method, and the *disputatio*, or disputation. The lecture method involved the professor reading the book to the students and the pupils carefully taking notes on the subject. The disputation was a series of statements, which the instructor placed in a common area for all students to see. After a week or so, the students would come to class and debate the statements. Many scholars believe that disputation is what Martin Luther did when he tacked his Ninety-Five Theses on the church door at Wittenburg.

The faculties consisted of instructors in arts, philosophy, and graduate studies in theology, law or medicine. During this period of history the greatest minds studied the Bible and theology. The medievalists considered theology as the "queen science". If one was not gifted enough to study theology he or she studied law. The lowliest profession was medicine because to practice it you had to get bloody. During the whole period, barbers performed surgery. This job requirement of the barber is why a barber's pole is white and red to signify bloody bandages. During the High Middle Ages when medical schools gave degrees, a law was passed in England which made it illegal for physicians to cut hair but not illegal for barbers to perform surgery.

The degrees offered were the bachelors, masters, and the doctorate. Instructors with doctoral degrees taught the masters degree students. Likewise, professors with masters degrees taught the bachelors degree students just as teaching assistants teach undergraduates today.

Debates Among Schoolmen

Schoolmen were scholars in the medieval universities. They constantly argued and debated each other in order to advance learning. The key debate of the period was the relationship of faith to reason: should a person accept things on faith alone or should one be able to reason things through to their logical conclusion? In sum, there were five viewpoints on the matter. The schoolman Berrenger suggested that the dogmas of the church could be explained through reason. Lanfranc stated that if reason and faith were in opposition, one should put the highest priority in faith. Averrores, the famous Islamic scholar, suggested that faith and reason are two different things and cannot be in opposition. Schoolman Aquinas believed that faith and reason are forms of truth. Since all truth is God's truth, they can never be in conflict with each other. Lastly, William of Ockham restated Averrores' contention that faith and reason are two separate forms of reality. He stated that it is like comparing apples and oranges, and there just is no sense in doing it. Ockham developed his "razor theory." This idea stated that the philosopher must cut out the philosophic ginger bread to the heart of the matter. That is what Ockham did in the faith to reason argument by concluding that the ideas operate in different spheres and are not in opposition to each other.

Humanism and Scholasticism

Francesco Petrarch was the intellectual founder of a paradigm of thought known as humanism. The cult of classical studies was the foundation of humanism in that Petrarch persisted in recapturing the essence of Greek and Roman times through literature. Humanism, the study of the world as it is, became a key ingredient in the manifestation of western culture.

Along with the rise of humanism came scholasticism. The logic of Aristotle used to prove church doctrines was significant in the movement of scholasticism. A pagan's philosophy used to explain Christian dogma was a revolutionary step toward the secularization of knowledge. Since pagan ideas could be used to explain church dogma, why not the universe itself? In this way, God could be taken out of the equation.

The first known scholastic was John of Salisbury who taught classical literature for its own value at Chartes Cathedral. Peter Abelard was perhaps one of the most gifted of the scholastics. He taught at the University of Paris and developed a method of discourse and rational interpretation, which set the form for teaching in the university. Albertus Magnus developed an experimental laboratory at the University of Cologne. Magnus was the mentor of Thomas Aquinas, the greatest of the scholastics. It was Saint Albertus who introduced Aristotle to Aquinas, enabling him to develop his logical proofs for the existence of God. Magnus's key scholarly contribution to Western learning was his synthesis of Neo-Platonic and Aristotelian ideas into a Christian paradigm.

The Christian paradigm of scholasticism reached its apex under the scholarship of Thomas Aquinas. In his greatest work, the *Summa Theologia*, Aquinas summarized all of learning and developed logical proofs for the existence of God in the *Prima Mobilia* argument. According to Aquinas, God is the Prime Mover (*Prima Mobilia*) of all movement in the universe. He also believed that the mind and God became one with intense study of theology and the classics. This mind meld with the deity has become known in philosophy and theology as the "Thomistic moment."

Legacy of the Medieval Universities

The modern university has developed customs, degrees and organizations that have their roots in the medieval university. Academic regalia are a product of the Middle Ages. Reverence for learning, professional studies and civilization itself are a legacy of the medieval universities.

Discussion Questions

1. Discuss the dualistic nature of medieval society.
2. Explain the tripartite system, the feudal contract, and subinfeudation.
3. Elaborate on the medieval pyramid.
4. How did the early history of the Franks tie them to Christianity?
5. Discuss the basic rudiments of the Carolingian Renaissance.
6. Frame the argument between Gregory VII and Henry IV.
7. What were the crusades?
8. What were the Seven Liberal Arts?
9. Compare and contrast chivalric and craft education.
10. Explain the medieval university in terms of methods, faculties and degrees.
11. Articulate the arguments among schoolmen.
12. Determine the significance of scholasticism and humanism by discussing key thinkers in those areas of thought.

References & Further Reading

Augustine. (1909) *Confessions*. New York: P.F. Collier & Son.

Brown, P.R.L.(1987) *Augustine of hippo: A biography*. New York: Dorset Press

Cantor, N.F. (1993) *The civilization of the middle ages*. New York: Harper.

Compayre, G. (1888) *History of pedagogy*. Boston: D.C. Heath.

Cubberley, E.P. (1948) *History of education: Educational practice and process-considered a phase of the development of western civilization*. New York: Houghton Mifflin

Daley, L. J. (1961) *The medieval university*. New York: Sheed & Ward.

Gaskoin, C.J.B. (1904) *Alcuin: His life and work*. London: Cambridge University Press.

Herlihy, David (1970) *The History of feudalism*. New York: Harper Collins.

MacKendrick, P., D. J. Genakoplos, J.H. Hexter, & R. Pipes. (1968) *Western civilization*. New York: Harper and Row

McKay, J. P., B.D. Hill & J. Buckler (1999) *A history of western society*. New York: Houghton Mifflin.

Power, E. (1991) *A legacy of learning: A history of western civilization*. Albany: State University of New York Press.

Wood, T.E. (2005) *How the catholic church built western civilization*, Washington, D.C.: Regenery Publishing.

Quintilian. (1905) *The institutes of oratory*. London: Dewick & Clark.

Chapter 6
The Renaissance and Reformation

Explain the significance of:

People: Jacob "the Rich" Fugger, Lorenzo "the Magnificent" de Medici, Francesco Petrarch, Dante, Boccaccio, Vittorino Feltre, Erasmus of Rotterdam, Niccolo Machiavelli, Johann Tetzel, Martin Luther, Pope Leo X, Charles V or II, Eck, Max Weber, Philip Melanchton, John Calvin, Henry VIII, Elizabeth I, Sir Thomas Moore, John Amos Komenský

Terms: Renaissance, usury, Hundred Years War, tripapacy, humanism, vernacular, reformation, "95 Theses", October 31, 1517, Diet of Worms, Weber thesis, vernacular school, Latin school, Church of England, counter-reformation, papal index, Dominicans, Jesuits

The Renaissance

Historical Overview

The Renaissance, meaning rebirth, began in the High Middle Ages and is considered the reawakening of Greco-Roman learning. The movement had its beginnings in Italy, especially in the city of Florence. Many changes occurred during the period that rushed in a large amount of modern paradigms of thought and action.

These paradigm shifts included the rise of banking and finance, which was prohibited for many years prior by the church's sin of usury. Usury was lending money for interest, which the church believed to be improper until the rise of banking families in Italy and Germany. These families were the Medici in Italy and the Fuggers in Germany. Jacob Fugger, known as "Jacob the Rich", gained so much money through lending funds to monarchs and Popes, that he could influence the course of history by choosing whom to loan money to. When he died, he had made more money than Bill Gates, the Microsoft tycoon, has today. Lorenzo "the Magnificent" de Medici was the banker in Italy. Both were patrons of great artists. For example, Lorenzo was the benefactor to both Michelangelo and Leonardo da Vinci. These financial geniuses opted for art that was in the Greco-Roman style rather than religious art. By their patronage, they secularized works of art.

Another change during the Renaissance was the rise of the nation-state brought about by the Hundred Years War, which gave the monarchs of both France and England the power to tax their subjects independent of the nobles. Therefore, monarchs could build standing armies and usurp more power for themselves. Powerful nations developed ruled by kings and queens. The rise of the nation-state caused a scramble for colonies that instigated the so-called Age of Discovery in which Europeans searched for an all water route to the East and in the process discovered new lands to dominate.

The wealth of city-states in Europe from trade with the East caused them to develop their own commerce. This rise of commerce led to a new class of people called the "*nouveaux riches*" or the "new rich" often referred to as the "bourgeoisie." These middle class people had money but no political power so they saw education as a means to social mobility. Therefore, they demanded schools for their children at government expense.

The medieval synthesis of the monolithic dominance of the Catholic Church eroded away due to these changes and various problems the church had during this era of change. The tripapacy with Popes in Rome, Avignon, and Pisa put a rift in the medieval fusion as symbolized in the Roman Church. The corruption of a number of high church officials and heretics also sent shock waves through Western society that caused new paradigms to emerge.

The Humanistic Educational Paradigm

Humanism and Vernacular Literature

Francesco Petrarch was the "Father of Humanism." He developed the study of the classics and wrote poetry in the vernacular. He said he was attempting to break bread with the dead in his efforts to recapture Greco-Roman learning.

Aside from Petrarch, the other literacy greats of the time were Dante and Boccaccio. Dante wrote *The Divine Comedy* and Boccaccio wrote *The Decameron*. Both works were written in the Tuscan dialect of Italian or the vernacular of the area in which they were published. Both works were written to entertain as well as inform. Vernacular literature was a major catalyst for literacy education. Once key works were available in their native tongue, people were motivated to learn how to read in order to enjoy the stories. Therefore, the humanistic paradigm consisted of studying the classics and the vernacular interpretation of the works through argument, composition, and debate.

Humanistic Teachers

One of the greatest of the humanist teacher was Vittorino Feltre. He was called the ablest of the new educators. He developed several teaching innovations which included physical education, games, individual differences, and the teacher-student relationship. Feltre believed that an educated person was in good health, had social graces, and was well rounded in all the arts. You might say this was his version of the Renaissance man (i.e. a man that can do everything well).

The epitome of the Renaissance man might very well have been Erasmus of Rotterdam. He was part of the Northern Renaissance because he came from the Netherlands. He wrote *In Praise of Folly* and *A Handbook of a Christian Knight*. Erasmus was able to be critical of the church without getting in trouble because he wrote fictional works. Historians believe that "Erasmus laid the egg that Luther hatched!" In other words, the logical end to Erasmus' arguments was revolt against the church, as Luther perceived it. Erasmus's pedagogical methods included classical studies, and a thorough analysis of each work, including moral and philosophical implications, the type of work, and a consideration for the author's bibliography. These ideas gave professors a template for teaching the classics.

Scholarship during the Renaissance branched out into new areas such as political science. Niccolo Machiavelli wrote extensively on politics producing two major treatises that are still being read and studied today. These works were *The Discourses* and *The Prince*. According to Machiavelli in these works, a republic is the best form of government if you can get it and if you can't you need a prince with no morals. His name has become associated with tyranny due to his writings in *The Prince*. In *The Discourses*, he advocated a representative democracy, but this has been overlooked. To really understand his ideas, both books, should be read together. Nonetheless, Machiavelli was the philosopher of *Realpolitik,* politics void of ethics. Modern rulers such as Mussolini and Hitler have embraced this approach to geo-politics.

Another area to make gains during the period of the Renaissance was women's education. Catherine of Sienna wrote a book titled: *The Book of Divine Doctrines*, and she actually started a school for women. Lucretia Borgia was influential in political affairs by articulating her socio-political opinions to the men in power. Lastly, Isabella d'Este patronized both male and female artists of the period, thereby giving patronage to the woman artisan.

The Reformation

Historical Overview

The Protestant Reformation was the revolt or protest against Catholic teaching by zealot reformers in the 16th Century. The catalyst for the movement was the selling of indulgences in Wittenburg, Germany by a monk, Johann Tetzel. Tetzel would say that every time a coin clings in his coffer, a soul is saved from purgatory and enters heaven. This upset a young monk who was a professor of moral philosophy at the University of Wittenburg named Martin Luther. He was livid because the poor people were buying indulgences instead of food. This led to his exercising his professorial duties and tacking the 95 Theses or statements on the church door. These statements were Luther's criticisms of the church and the sale of indulgences. In doing so, Luther was using the pedagogical technique of the disputation or *disputatio*. The document was posted in a place so that the students could debate the ideas in class with the professor at a later date. Things got out of hand, and the result was the Protestant Reformation. Luther, seeing an opportunity to lead a movement, decided to see what would happen next.

The events of October 31, 1517, or the tacking of the disputation got Luther in trouble with Pope Leo X, his monarch Charles V of the Holy Roman Empire, and his prince, Frederick of Saxony. The Pope made Charles V call a meeting at the city of Worms to have Luther debate his ideas against Eck, the Papal master scholar and theologian of the day.

Charles V, king of Germany was also Charles I of Spain. He had nothing but ill will for his German holdings. He would often say: "I speak French to my women, Spanish to my soldiers and German to my horse!" The Pope ordered Charles to preside over the debate between Luther and Eck. The Diet or Assembly of Worms met and the two scholars debated.

In the end, Luther was asked to take back roughly 14 of the 95 Theses. At this point he refused saying, "Here I stand, I cannot do otherwise!" At that moment, the Pope excommunicated Luther. This was the greatest punishment bestowed upon a person. Luther was a person outside the law, an outlaw. He was in danger but his prince, Frederick of Saxony, offered him sanctuary in his castle. While safe in Frederick's castle, he translated the Bible into German. Luther hoped that a vernacular Bible would lead to greater literacy among the peasants.

Luther's Theology and Educational Ideas

Luther's theology was based on the writings of Saint James and the passage: "The just shall live by faith alone!" The Catholic Church believed that one needed faith and good works to enter heaven. Luther, on the other hand, espoused that faith alone was necessary for salvation. Luther developed the ideas of universal literacy, vocations (i.e. religious, political, and domestic or economic), and the Protestant work ethic, which was the idea that hard work leads to success in any endeavor. Max Weber developed the "Weber thesis" which stated that capitalism and Protestantism developed together because of Luther's notions about vocations and work ethic.

Philip Melanchton was a humanistic scholar who advised Luther on educational matters. According to Melanchton, the object of education was to create educated citizens who recognized authority, who were trained craftsman, and who could make positive contributions to society. Luther and Melanchton created mass education throughout Germany. The vernacular schools were to provide literacy enabling everyone to read the Bible in German, the native tongue. The gymnasiums, or secondary schools, were for older students to prepare for the university. Therefore, mass literacy education begins with Luther.

Calvinism and Education

Once Luther made his break with the Roman Church, other reformers came to the forefront, in particularly John Calvin. Calvin developed his theology based two doctrines: stewardship and human depravity. Stewardship called upon followers to be frugal and not waste resources that others might use in the future. People had to care about future generations. Human depravity was based on the original sin doctrine that all humans are innately evil, so religion is necessary to make them good. Through prayer and worship, people could be made right. Calvin used his theology to create a dual track educational system. A vernacular school for the common people, a Latin school for the rich people, and a classical secondary school for those elect who would go on to higher learning. According to Calvin, most people needed basic literacy in order to read the Bible, but a few "Elect of God" needed further education because they were chosen to be leaders and predestined to get to heaven. How did Calvin know who were the Elect? The rich, of course. God gave them money, so they had to be the chosen few to get into paradise. This is evidence of the Weber Thesis that Protestantism and capitalism helped each other in their developmental phases.

The Anglican Reformation

The church in England was a mainstay of Catholicism so much so that the Pope named Henry VIII "Defender of the Faith" for keeping Protestantism out of the British Isles. Henry VIII was obsessed with primogeniture, he needed a male heir to pass his kingdom on to. This caused him no end of grief because his wife Catherine had a daughter. Ironically, this girl became one of England's greatest monarchs, Elizabeth I.

Henry decided he needed a different wife, so he petitioned the Papacy to annul his marriage to Catherine who was from Spain. The Pope was inclined to grant his request for annulment because he personally liked Henry and he wanted to keep England in the Roman Church. Philip II, King of Spain was outraged because Henry's wife was his aunt. Philip II threatened to destroy Vatican City if the Pope granted the petition, so the Holy Father refused to allow the annulment of Henry's marriage.

The Pope's action on the petition prompted Henry to create the Church of England or the Anglican Church. Henry had six wives and only one son, Edward, who died when he was fourteen. Henry forced all the nobles and clergy in England to sign the Act of Supremacy that made the king the head of church and state. Sir Thomas Moore, author of the book *Utopia*, refused to sign the Act and was sent to prison for years and then was killed on Henry's orders. This was unfortunate because Moore was a brilliant scholar and a dear friend to Henry. Henry's obsession with primogeniture was more important than friendship itself.

The Catholic Counter Reformation

The Roman Church attempted to reform itself in the guise of the Counter-Reformation. The basic teachings of the church were reaffirmed at the Council of Trent. For example, the council created the *papal index* which was a list of books that good Catholics were not to read, such as certain works by Aristotle, Galileo, and Luther. In modern times, the works of Darwin, Freud, and Voltaire were added to the list of condemned books.

In addition, a number of holy orders of friars began to teach. In particular, the Dominicans built houses of study in every major city of Europe. It was thought by the church fathers that education would be the key to combating Protestantism.

A leader arose who would be considered the Catholic Luther: Ignatius of Loyola. He founded the Jesuits who are sometimes referred to as "The Pope's Marines" because they were always the first to defend the church from heretics. The Jesuits built universities all over the world. Jesuit education consisted of the study of humane letters, natural science, and theology. Their pedagogy was repetition, written exercise, oral and public examination, and dictation. Today, Jesuit universities such as Loyola of Chicago and New Orleans are major institutions of higher learning in America.

John Amos Komenský

This historical period can be summed up in the work of John Amos Komenský, or Comenius, who was a Protestant realist educator. He believed that the purpose of education was to prepare people for the future. He rejected corporal punishment. Comenius hypothesized correctly that the general patterns of human development were the basis of education. These ideas have become a part of the Western educational tradition.

Discussion Questions

1. What changes eroded the medieval synthesis?
2. Explain the humanistic educational paradigm.
3. Discuss the ideas of the humanistic teachers.
4. What were the causes of the Protestant Reformation and the Catholic Counter-Reformation?
5. What were Luther's educational ideas?
6. Explain Calvin's educational ideas.
7. How was the Anglican reformation different from Luther's revolt?
8. Explain the major tenets of the Catholic Counter-Reformation.
9. What were the ideas of Comenius?

References & Further Reading

Comenius, J.A. (1896) *The great didactic.* London: Adam and Black

Compayre, G. (1888) *History of pedagogy.* Boston: D.C. Heath.

Cubberley, E.P. (1948) *History of education: Educational practice and process considered a phase of the development of western civilization.* New York: Houghton Mifflin

MacKendrick, P., D. J. Genakoplos, J.H. Hexter, & R. Pipes. (1968) *Western civilization.* New York: Harper and Row

McKay, J. P., B.D. Hill & J. Buckler (1999) *A history of western society.* New York: Houghton Mifflin.

Moore, Paul (1905) *History of education.* New York: MacMillan

Van Doren, Charles (1991). *A history of knowledge: Past, present, and future* New York: Ballantine Books.

Wood, T.E. (2005) *How the catholic church built western civilization.* Washington, D.C.: Regenery Publishing.

Chapter 7
The Enlightenment

Explain the significance of:

People: Copernicus, Galileo, Tycho Brahe, Johann Kepler, Isaac Newton, Jean Jacques Rousseau, John Locke, Johann Pestalozzi, Johann Herbart

Terms: heliocentric theory, natural laws, gravitation, calculus, *Emile*, negative education

Paradigm Shift: The Scientific Revolution

Due to the upheavals caused by the Renaissance and Reformation, the medieval synthesis of knowledge grounded in faith was destroyed and scholars began to apply science and reason to solve problems. This is known as a paradigm shift or revolution, which is any fundamental change in thinking. The first area to feel the impact of the new ideas was science. The key scientist of the epoch was Copernicus, who developed the heliocentric theory of the universe. During the medieval period, the church scholars accepted the ancients' theory of an earth-centered universe. Copernicus, a Polish astronomer, hypothesized that the sun was the center of the universe in his heliocentric theory. This revelation destroyed the medieval synthesis of a God-created universe with His greatest creation, man at the center.

Galileo, using a telescope that he improved, proved Copernicus correct but the inquisition forced him to recant, or take back his findings. Other thinkers of the age were Tycho Brahe and Johann Kepler who made contributions in physics. However, the scientific giant of the age was Sir Isaac Newton. He believed that natural laws governed the universe, and that the scientific method could be applied to solve problems in science as well as society. Newton postulated that the philosophers' task was to adjust society to natural law. Newton was most famous for his hypothesis on gravitation, and his development of calculus.

Paradigm Shift: Religious, Political, and Social

The scientific paradigm shift gave way to changing ideas in the social sciences and religion. Deism became the religious belief of the Enlightenment. This concept held that God was the primary mover in the universe, and that the universe was like a clock, which God wound up and let go. A clockwork universe was agreeable to scientists but allowed for no divine intervention and that perplexed theologians.

The thinkers of the age wrote on the topics of politics and adjusting society to natural laws. Among these theorists were John Locke and Jean Jacques Rousseau. John Locke wrote *An Essay Concerning Human Understanding*. In this work Locke suggested that people construct their own knowledge based on experience. Jean Jacques Rousseau illustrated this idea of experiential education in his book *Emile: On Education*.

In this treatise, Rousseau stated that humans were fundamentally free and that society corrupted people. He developed a formula for education that was centered on progressive developmental learning. Rousseau advocated natural education, which moved to permissiveness in child rearing. He suggested developmental sequential learning and negative education. Negative education was learning from ones mistakes. For example, if a small child touched something hot and got burned, he or she would learn not to do that again. Rousseau believed that books were corrupting and would not have any in early education. The only book he would allow Emile to read was Daniel Defoe's *Robinson Caruso* because it was a story about a man and his relationship with nature.

The Legacy of the Enlightenment

The Age of Reason, or the Enlightenment, has left an enduring legacy on education in Western society. The period was complex historically with a mixture of neoclassical rationalism and romantic idealism. The way modern civilization views childhood changed as a result of the philosophies. Childhood was now seen as a developmental period of innocence in which the child was nurtured instead of beaten or ignored.

Johann Pestalozzi and Johann Herbart were two key educational reformers who came from the tradition of the Enlightenment. Both developed humane, nurturing, natural, and scientific principles of education that had an impact on the education of today's students.

Discussion Questions

1. Explain the paradigm shift brought about by the scientific revolution.
2. Explain the paradigm shift brought about by the religious, political and social revolutions.
3. Discuss Rousseau's thoughts on naturalism.
4. What was the legacy of the enlightenment?
5. Who were Herbart and Pestalozzi?

References & Further Reading

Cubberley, E.P. (1948) *History of education; Educational practice and process considered a phase of the development of western civilization.* New York: Houghton Mifflin

Kuhn, T. (1957) *The copernican revolution; Planetary astronomy in the development of western thought.* Cambridge: Harvard University Press.

McKay, J. P., B.D. Hill & J. Buckler (1999) *A history of western society.* New York: Houghton Mifflin.

Power, E. J. (1991) *A legacy of learning; A history of western civilization.* Albany: State University of New York Press

Chapter 8
Democratic Revolutionary Education: America & France

Explain the significance of:

People: Horace Mann, Benjamin Rush, Benjamin Franklin, Thomas Jefferson, Metternich, Napoleon Bonaparte, King Louis XVI, Marquis de Condorcet, Robespierre

Terms: *Old Satan Deluder Law*, dame school, hornbook, sampler, early national period, common school, Northwest Ordinance, Northwest Territory, "Reserve Clause", "Bill for the More General Diffusion of Knowledge". "An Aristocracy of the Intellect", thermordorian reaction, "The Little Corporal", Jacobins, Decree of School Organization

Historical Overview of American Education

Prior to contemporary times (cr. 1870) there were three periods of American educational history: the colonial, the early national, and the common school eras. The colonial period was from 1607 to 1775. During this, time, the first educational legislation was passed in New England, the *Old Satan Deluder Law*. This law stated that idle hands were the devil's workshop, thereby setting the purpose of education as religious. Keep the children busy and teach them to read the Bible. This law actually planted the seed for public education in the future. Religion was the core curriculum and education, for the most part, was for wealthy men. Girls and boys might have gone to a dame school. A dame school was run by a local woman who would teach the girls domestic skills and the boys to read using a hornbook that was somewhat like a clipboard covered by a clear sheet of animal horn. The boys went on to secondary school and the girls made a sampler. The sampler was their diploma because it was evidence that they knew their ABCs and the domestic arts because they sewed the sampler.

The period from 1775 to 1820 was known as the early national period. Education took on some modern characteristics such as separation of church and state as well as state control. The purpose of education at this time became nation building.

The third era was that of the common school which was from 1820 to 1880. Due to the work of Horace Mann, schools become standardized with desks, blackboards, and books. Tax support for elementary schools became common. Grade levels were established and normal schools, or teacher's colleges, were created. The school was referred to as a "common school" because anyone could attend.

Education in the United States: Legal Foundations

Prior to the framing of the United States Constitution, the only achievement of our first government under the Articles of Confederation was the Northwest Ordinance in 1785. This document dealt with the so-called "Northwest Territory" and was developed for orderly settlement in what became the states of Michigan, Wisconsin, Indiana, Illinois, and Ohio.

This law was significant because it stipulated that when a community reached a certain size it had to set aside land and provide for a school. This was the only mention of education in any early government document and it set the legal precedent for public support of elementary education.

After the ratification of the Constitution by the various states, reformers looked to the 10th Amendment to the Constitution or the "reserve clause" to sanction public support and local control of education. The reserve clause stated that the powers not delegated to the federal government were reserved for the states and the people. Since education is not mentioned in the constitution, it is a power reserved for the states and local communities.

Educational Proposals during the Revolutionary Period

Many people proposed educational plans during the U.S. revolutionary period. Prominent educational templates came from Benjamin Rush, Benjamin Franklin, and Thomas Jefferson.

Benjamin Rush was a physician who believed that education should be an instrument of nation building. According to him, the role of education should be to develop scientific attitudes and promote progress.

Benjamin Franklin's proposal included a practical curriculum of English, grammar and the classics. He believed that schooling should lead to practical pursuits and therefore be utilitarian in scope.

If anyone should be called the "Father of American Education" it should be Thomas Jefferson because he actually submitted an education bill to the Virginia Assembly, which was defeated on several occasions. Jefferson's "Bill for the More General Diffusion of Knowledge," called for both egalitarian means and intellectual rewards. Based on the bill, elementary schools would be state-funded and open to everyone. These schools would deliver instruction in reading, writing, arithmetic, and history. Those who made good grades would go on to a grammar school, which was a secondary school that taught Latin, Greek, English, geography, and higher mathematics. Those who excelled in this school would go on to college and graduate school at state expense. Once they graduated, the former students would become government officials and give back to the state through service. Jefferson was influenced by Plato's concept of the philosopher-king. Essentially, he advocated "An Aristocracy of the Intellect."

Accordingly, frontier agrarian egalitarianism caused education in a democratic culture to have two roles. One role was to provide common core knowledge to relate to the masses. The other role was to identify the talented and prepare them to assume leadership. Republican education was seen as a civic, political, and social instrument deliberately designed to advance democratic skills, values, and knowledge.

Educational Ideas during the French Revolution and the Napoleonic Reign

The Austrian diplomat Metternich once said: "Whenever France sneezes Europe catches a cold!" There is no better historical illustration of that than the French Revolution and the rise of the "Little Corporal" Napoleon Bonaparte. The symbol of the revolt was the storming of the Bastille, a debtors' prison. After the fall of King Louis XVI, the radical Jacobins, under Robespierre, gained power and instituted changes in the entire nation including educational reforms. The Jacobin Assembly passed the Decree of School Organization in 1795. This law called for an educational system for France which included: a primary school that was a home or private instruction, a secondary school that taught languages, drawing, natural history, sciences, literature, grammar, history, and law, and lastly, a polytechnical school to educate civil and military engineers.

Marquis de Condorcet was chosen as the Minister of Education. His philosophy of education suggested that knowledge was a product of sensory experience. He was a student of the Enlightenment and an advocate of science and progress. According to Condorcet, science secured progressive development in society. Therefore, his plan for education called for the state to provide equality of education through universally public supported schools in order to ensure progress.

Napoleonic Educational Paradigms

Through a series of events that led to a thermordorian reaction (i.e. a conservative reaction after a radical period of time), which brought about the execution of the Jacobin's leader Robespierre, Napoleon became the emperor of the French. As most tyrants, Napoleon realized that in order to maintain his power he had to control the education of the young.

Napoleon created the imperial university in 1808 to oversee the institutions of learning in France. A grand master was put in charge of the schools. Napoleon let the churches run the primary schools. He gave the secondary schools his priority. French secondary schools during the imperial reign of the "Little Corporal" consisted of *lycees* that were boarding schools with a six year curriculum of the classics and mathematics, *instituts* that were independently-run schools, and colleges that were municipal schools run by various cities and villages. Higher education focused on theology, law, medicine, science, and the arts. In addition, Napoleon had three prestigious institutions that would train the professional elite for government service. These were the *Ecole Militaire* for military officers, the *Ecole Normale Superieure* for professors, and the *Ecole Polytechnique* for engineers. Napoleon believed that education was meant to train citizens to do their duty. Therefore, he set a pattern of centralization and repression of intellectual thought so much so that he outlined the curriculum right down to the minutes and hours of the study of each proscribed subject.

The Historical Legacy of the Revolutionary Age

The American and French Revolutions sought to give concrete political and social expression to the ideas of the Enlightenment. These two paradigm shifts had a profound effect on educational change in the West. As a result of these upheavals, education was tied to the cultivation of nationalism among the youth, who were destined to be the citizens, leaders, scholars, and soldiers of the nation-states in which they resided.

Discussion Questions

1. What was the *Old Satan Deluder Law*?
2. Discuss the curriculum in a dame school.
3. What were the three period of educational history in the United States?
4. Explore the legal foundations of education in the United States.
5. Articulate the educational proposals from the American revolutionary period.
6. Discuss the educational ideas from the French revolutionary period and the Napoleonic reign.
7. What was the educational legacy from the revolutionary age?

References & Further Reading

Addams, J. (1985) *Jane addams on education.* New York: Teachers College Press.

Cubberley, E.P. (1948) *History of education: Educational practice and process considered a phase of the development of western civilization.* New York: Houghton Mifflin.

Good, H.G. (1962) *A history of american education.* Boston: D.C. Heath.

McKay, J. P., B.D. Hill & J. Buckler (1999) *A history of western society.* New York: Houghton Mifflin.

Power, E. J. (1991) *A legacy of learning: A history of western civilization.* Albany: State University of New York Press.

Tarnas, Richard (1991) *The passion of the western mind: Understanding the ideas that have shaped our world view.* New York: Ballantine Books.

Van Doren, Charles (1991). *A history of knowledge: Past, present, and future.* New York: Ballantine Books.

Wood, T.E. (2005) *How the catholic church built western civilization.* Washington, D.C.: Regenery Publishing.

Chapter 9
Reformers: Paradigm Realities of the New Educators

Explain the significance of:

People: John Amos Komenský, Johann Heinrich Pestalozzi, Frederick Froebel, Edward Sheldon, Joseph McClue, Joseph Neef, Robert Owen, Johann Herbart

Terms: object lesson, *Leonard and Gertrude*, *How Gertrude Teaches Her Children*, *Anschauung*, New Harmony, Oswego Normal School, Herbartian method

The New Educators

Key individual reformers have left a legacy to American education during the various periods of history discussed in this book from the beginning with the Enlightenment to the current age. They worked to created schools and learning philosophies based on empirical data and observation. These so-called "New Educators" included John Amos Komenský, Johann Heinrich Pestalozzi, Frederick Froebel, Joseph Neef, Henry Barnard, Edward Sheldon, Mary Sheldon Barnes, and Johann Herbart.

John Amos Komenský

John Amos Komensky, better known in the West as "Comenius," was a protestant realist who rejected corporal punishment and proposed a pedagogy that was based on the general patterns of human development. He also put forth the radical notion that education should prepare students for the future by studying subjects of practical application to contemporary society such as science and math.

Johann Heinrich Pestalozzi

Johann Heinrich Pestalozzi was a Swiss educational reformer who might be regarded as the "Father of Early Childhood Education." He created, ran, and taught in three schools, the farm at Neudorf, the orphanage at Stanz, and the castle at Burgdorf. Pestalozzi believed that all children should be taught, so he worked with the poorest of children, orphans, and had many financial difficulties as a result. He developed many pedagogical innovations such as simultaneous instruction and the "object lesson." The "object lesson" was the key to his whole theory of instruction. Pestalozzi believed that an object from nature such as an apple or a plant could be used to teach all subjects without textbooks. The object could be touched, seen, smelled, and sometimes tasted. The students could experience the object with their senses.

According to Pestalozzi, each object had a specific form or shape, and number or quantity (weight). Using an apple, a teacher could deliver instruction in geometry by discussing shape, science by discussing how we grow apples and even history by talking about William Tell or Isaac Newton. Pestalozzi's teaching style consisted of no corporal punishment, developmental instruction, and no rote memorization. When discussing objects, he would proceed from near to far, simple to complex, and specific to general.

Pestalozzi elucidated these ideas in two books *How Gertrude Teaches Her Children* and *Leonard and Gertrude*. The schoolmaster used the term *Anschauung* to mean when the student got it, or the "aha" phenomena. He believed that sensation was the key to learning. Accordingly, a model for instruction emerges in Pestalozzi's pedagogy: first is the object followed by drawing then doing and lastly reading.

Pestalozzi's Disciples

Pestalozzi's students spread his pedagogy to America and other lands in both Europe and Asia. Among these disciples was Frederick Froebel who developed Kindergarten. Froebel studied with Pestalozzi and modified the object lesson by creating the ten gifts. The ten gifts were manipulatives, which could be used to teach children multidisciplinary lessons.

Another pupil of Pestalozzi was Joseph Neef. Neef demonstrated the "object lesson" at the World's Fair in London where Edward Sheldon and Joseph McClue saw it and were so impressed they asked Neef to come to America and instruct teachers on the pedagogy. Neef brought the "object lesson" to America and McClue was instrumental in getting Robert Owen to use Pestalozzian pedagogy in the schools at New Harmony, Indiana. Edward Sheldon was the principal of Oswego Normal School in New York and he made Pestalozzi's ideas a vital part of the teacher education curriculum at that institution. Graduates from Oswego were hired by normal schools across the United States. In fact, two Oswego graduates were hired at the Normal School at Slippery Rock, Pennsylvania to be professors of Pedagogy. Therefore there is a direct link from Normal Schools in various states to Pestalozzi.

Johann Herbart

Johann Herbart was a student of Pestalozzi's and took the "object lesson" one step further by adding reading courses to the curriculum, particularly literature and history. Herbart is also credited with the application of science to pedagogy. He developed the Herbartian Teaching Method. This technique included five steps:

1) Preparation: Preparing the student to receive a new idea.
2) Presentation: Presenting the student with the new idea.
3) Association: Assimilating the new idea with the old ideas.
4) Generalization: The general idea deriving from the combination of old and new ideas.
5) Application: Applying the new information.

In many ways, Herbart's template for instruction is very similar to the 5E method utilized in science pedagogy today.

Discussion Questions

1. Discuss the pedagogical ideas of:
   a. John Amos Komenský
   b. Johann Heinrich Pestalozzi
   c. Frederick Froebel
   d. Joseph Neef
   e. Johann Herbart
2. How did Pestalozzianism get to America?
3. Why was the Oswego Normal School significant?

References & Further Reading

Cubberley, E.P. (1948) *History of education: Educational practice and process considered a phase of the development of western civilization.* New York: Houghton Mifflin

Comenius, J.A. (1896) *The great didactic.* London: Adam and Black.

Froebel, F. (1887) *The education of man.* New York: Appleton.

Herbart, J.F. (1901) *Outlines of educational doctrine.* New York: MacMillan.

MacKendrick, P., D. J. Genakoplos, J.H. Hexter, & R. Pipes. (1968) *Western civilization.* NewYork: Harper and Row

McKay, J. P., B.D. Hill & J. Buckler (1999) *A history of western society.* New York: Houghton Mifflin.

Pestalozzi, J.H. (1951) *The education of man-aphorisms.* New York: Philosophical Library

Power, E. J. (1991) *A legacy of learning: A history of western civilization.* Albany: State University of New York Press.

Tarnas, Richard (1991) *The passion of the western mind: Understanding the ideas that have shaped our world view.* New York: Ballantine Books.

Van Doren, Charles (1991). *A history of knowledge: Past, present, and future.* New York: Ballantine Books.

Wood, T.E. (2005) *How the catholic church built western civilization.* Washington, D.C.: Regenery Publishing.

Chapter 10
The 19ᵗʰ Century

Explain the significance of:

People: Edmund Burke, John Stuart Mill, Jeremy Bentham, Charles Fourier, Karl Marx, Frederick Hegel, Johann Herder, Johann Fichte, Charles Darwin, John Dewey, Herbert Spencer, William Graham Sumner, Andrew Carnegie, John D. Rockfeller, Sigmund Freud, Horace Mann, Henry Barnard, Abraham Lincoln, Edward Sheldon, Prudence Crandell, Emma Willard

Terms: "Age of Isms", conservatism, *Reflections on the French Revolution*, conservatism, liberalism, socialism, utopian socialism, "Butterfly Theory", New Harmony, *Das Kapital*, class struggle, Marxism, nationalism, "Social Darwinism", psychoanalysis, defense mechanisms, common school, Latin Grammar School, Morrill Land Grant Act, *Kalamazoo Case*, normal schools, Oswego Normal School, Committee of 10, "Cult of Domesticity", seminaries

An Age of Isms

The 19th Century was said to be the "Age of 'Isms" or the "Ideological Century." Both are true to some extent. An ideology is an abstract construct of socio-political philosophy that guides practical activities and political groups' actions. The leading ideologies of the 19th Century were: conservatism, liberalism, socialism, Marxism, and nationalism.

Conservatism

Conservative thought is derived from the ideas of the British philosopher, Edmund Burke. He developed his theories after the trauma of the French

Revolution. In response to this devastation to the status quo, Burke wrote *The Reflections on the French Revolution.* He believed that stability in government and society was necessary for a culture to be maintained.

In France, the Jacobins changed everything, including such things as the months and the days of the week. This was merely change for changes sake and that innovation was nauseating to a conservative who wanted to maintain the status quo. This may have influenced Burke, who believed in freedom from government or negative government. It was his contention that the government should stay out of peoples' lives and that individuals should be free to pursue their own interests. The state should not mandate personal behavior. Burke wanted to get government out of citizens' lives as much as possible. He believed that the state should provide education but not require attendance. To Burke, education was an attempt to transmit culture not to change society. Burke's conservatism rejected school as an agent for change and viewed school an agency to preserve the status quo.

Basic conservative principles are stable and traditional institutions, restraint on human behavior, and a conventional education system. The conservatives value churches as primary educators because they preach morals.

Liberalism

Liberalism stemmed from the Enlightenment and the developing middle class. Liberals believe in the freedom of speech, press, and assembly. They oppose authoritarian governments and state churches. Key liberals were John Stuart Mill and Jeremy Bentham. Mill wrote on individual liberty in *On Liberty* and Bentham on utilitarianism in *The Calculus.* These theorists believed that government ought to make a good society and education should be used as a vehicle for social change.

Socialism

Socialism was a response to industrialization. According to Webster's Dictionary, socialism is any of various economic and political theories advocating collective or governmental ownership and administration of the means of production and distribution of goods. Charles Fourier was an Utopian Socialist who believed that ideal working communities of 1000 people could be created, but not whole utopian cultures or societies. The most interesting aspect of Fourier's scheme of communities was his "butterfly theory." This was his belief that variety was the spice of life so no one should do any work for more than two hours at any given job. Someone could be a farmer, a boss, a teacher, and a lawyer in an eight-hour work day, however, the educational limits to this would make it almost unworkable. Robert Owen put some of Fourier's ideas into practice when he created his ideal workers' communities at New Harmony, Indiana and in Scotland. Owen also developed schools in his communities based on the ideas of the Swiss pedagogical reformer Pestalozzi.

Marxism

Scientific socialism was a type of socialism that was created by Karl Marx. Marx believed that he had found laws of history and society that were similar to laws of nature. Marx developed his ideas in his magnum opus *Das Kapital* or *On Capital*. In this work, he put forth his concepts of economic causation, class struggle, the Theory of Surplus Value, bloody revolution, and the withering away of the state.

To sum up his ideas, Marx believed that all change in history was a result of economics and nothing else. He stated that a class struggle existed between the have and have-nots, and this conflict would lead to a bloody revolution and an eventual workers' paradise. There would be a brief period of workers' rule to make society good, and once that was accomplished, the state would wither away and a blissful anarchy would take its place. People would live by the credo: "From each according to their abilities, to each according to their needs."

Nationalism

Nationalism is a sense of state consciousness exalting one's country above all others and placing prime prominence on endorsement of its civilization, culture, and welfare as opposed to those of other nations or supranational groups. This extreme love of one's country can grow into extremism, leading to wars and pogroms of genocide.

Frederick Hegel and Johann Herder, two German philosophers of the 19th Century, came to believe that every nation possessed a *Volksgeist* or *folk spirit*. Johann Fichte, another German philosopher believed that the German *Volksgeist* was superior, thus starting the myth of German racial and physical superiority that became so terrible during the Nazi reign.

Darwin, Science, and Society

Charles Darwin wrote *The Origin of the Species*, published in 1859. In that book, Darwin used science to explain the theory of evolution. His major premise was that ape and humans had a common ancestor. This destroyed the theological interpretation of the beginnings of humankind. After this time, the cult of science was used to define the world rather than philosophy or theology. These changes in thought would also alter the principles of teaching and learning. After 1859 AD, epistemology, the philosophy that studies the nature of human knowledge, was altered. This in turn changed what was taught and learned.

Since Darwin, many theorists such as William James and G. Stanley Hall believed that the application of science could solve all the world's problems. John Dewey developed a whole philosophy of pedagogy based on the scientific principles of experiment and observation.

Darwin's key concepts were "the survival of the fittest," and "adaptation to the environment." Darwin believed that weaker species died out over time and the stronger ones survived and reproduced. Thus the concept of "the survival of the fittest" was born. Darwin also stated that the smartest creatures learned and adapted from their environments.

Many theorists of the 19th Century took these ideas of Darwin and applied them to society. These ideas became a philosophy know as "social Darwinism." The two most dominant thinkers in this paradigm of thought were Herbert Spencer and William Graham Sumner. Herbert Spencer was the founder of the movement and its intellectual guru. He developed a cult following of robber barons such as Andrew Carnegie and John D. Rockefeller who believed they were the fittest because they were rich. Spencer wrote a book on education entitled: *What Knowledge is Most Worth Knowing*. This work had a profound effect on education in both Europe and the United States. Spencer stated that education should be practical and concern itself with teaching students self-preservation, parenting skills, social and political relationships, the necessities of life, as well as leisure activities. William Graham Sumner brought Spencer's ideas to America and they took root here among the intellectuals of the 19th Century. Sumner believed competition was the key to a society's greatness. He advocated a hierarchy in society and the utility of poverty.

Freud and Education

Sigmund Freud created a body of knowledge and therapeutic techniques known as psychoanalysis. Freud believed that humans were not rational, thinking beings. He asserted that unconscious forces sometimes motivate people. In order to understand this concept, Freud created a schema of personality. This structure consisted of the id, ego, and superego. The id was the individual's basic drives and was governed by the "pleasure principle"(people seek pleasure and avoid pain). The ego was governed by social norms. Finally, the superego was the moral sense in the personality. For example, The id would direct a person to do what they want to do, the ego would direct a person to do what they had to do, and the superego would direct a person to do the right thing.

Freud believed that the unconscious ruled a person psychologically. Therefore, he developed techniques to reach the unconscious and this became psychoanalysis. According to Freud, dreams are manifestations from beyond consciousness and they must be understood two ways: manifest and latent content. Manifest content was the straight story line of the dream and latent content was the hidden symbolic meaning of the dream, a message from the subconscious level in the id. One of the more interesting paradigms developed by Freud was the idea of the defense mechanism. If the body had defenses against diseases, than Freud hypothesized that the mind had to possess defenses against strong emotional hurts. Some examples of these defenses would be repression, which is the automatic act of forgetting an unpleasant experience; regression, which is going back to more infantile behavior for security; sublimation, which is expressing an antisocial behavior in a socially acceptable way; or reaction formation, which is taking the opposite view of how we really feel. Freud's legacy to education is his belief that childhood is an important period of life and in school children may be acting out problems that go beyond the classroom.

American Education in the 19th Century

Common Schools

The common school was the primary educational institution in the United States during the 19th Century. The basic curriculum consisted of the three "Rs": reading, writing, and arithmetic. The word "common" was used to signify that the school was open to all students and civil education was stressed. The common school movement lasted from 1820 to 1880. The New England model for the common school was adopted throughout the nation because Massachusetts was the first state to develop public education based on the common school model. As the country expanded westward, schools developed along the New England common school template.

Due to the work of Horace Mann, schools become standardized with desks, blackboards, and books. Tax support for elementary schools became common. Grade levels were established and the normal schools, or teachers' colleges, were created. In 12 Annual Reports, Mann, the first State Secretary of Education for the State of Massachusetts, laid out the model for how schools would later be set up in America. Mann believed that public funding was necessary for the Republic to be maintained by educated citizens.

Most children went to school in the 19th Century if they could physically get to the school. Hardly any states provided a common school education, but in local towns and villages, churches and citizens developed schools. The teachers were free to do as they pleased until after the Civil War when the curriculum became somewhat more standardized. The agricultural society determined school schedules, and children were excused from school during the spring and summer for planting and harvesting. The contemporary paradigm of summer vacation is a legacy from our agrarian past.

Common school teaching methods were dictated by time. The teacher had to race through the curriculum using the same method for all students. Pupils would be clustered into groups of four or five and read aloud from one book in round-robin fashion. This was called "say your lessons." This was employed with any subject that required reading. According to one schoolmaster from New York City in 1900, the basic method of instruction in reading subjects was to give the students an outline and assign lessons with oral instruction and a written exercise at the end of the week.

Testing in the common school was done by having students "toe the line." The teacher would quiz each student by having them put their toes on a line in the front of the classroom near the teacher's desk and answer questions. If they got the question right, they could sit down. If they got the question wrong, they could be swatted with a hickory switch or made to sit in a corner with a "dunce" cap on.

Henry Barnard was another important reformer on the American scene during this period of time. He created the public school movement in Connecticut. Barnard developed a framework of tax support for public education. He is also known as the "Father of the American high school." Barnard started the Latin Grammar School, which was the first high school in the United States. However, the oldest secondary school in America is the English Classic School in Boston, which opened in 1821.

In 1862, Abraham Lincoln signed the Morrill Land Grant Act which set up land grant colleges across the country such as The Pennsylvania State University and Ohio State University. These colleges would help farmers develop scientific methods of farming and would be open to the children of the working class.

Government support for both elementary schools and higher education had come to pass in the 19th century. However, it wasn't until the latter half of the century that tax support for secondary education came about as a result of the *Kalamazoo Case*. This was a Supreme Court decision in which the court ruled in favor of the city government taxing its residents to pay for a high school in the community. By the end of the century, local, state, and federal governments funded every level of education. Teacher education also became a priority of the states with the introduction of normal schools by such reformers as Horace Mann and Edward Sheldon. They were called normal schools because they had norms or standards. Normal schools trained teachers for the one-room schoolhouses throughout the nation.

Normal Schools

The first normal schools were established in the United States around 1823. The curriculum consisted of a two-year course of study. Most students entered the school after elementary school and a high school certificate was not needed for matriculation. Students reviewed elementary curricula and took secondary school courses such as history and science as well as some classes in "pedagogy." A high school diploma was not required for normal school admittance until 1900. Interestingly, some high schools in isolated or rural areas were normal schools because they prepared school teachers and in that respect they were the first vocational schools because they produced people for a specific job, teaching.

A teacher training institution, Slippery Rock State Normal School, during the fall term of 1894, offered courses in the following subjects: physiology, hygiene, geography, United States history, the art and science of teaching, school management, psychology, methods of teaching, history of education, general history, world history, natural science, plane geometry, rhetoric, composition,

English literature, Latin, and physical culture. This curriculum prepared the students to teach in the schools.

The Normal School in Oswego, New York was the prototype for normal schools in America. Its principal, Edward Sheldon, adopted Pestalozzian and Herbartian principles of pedagogy into the curriculum. As you recall, these principles espoused the "object lesson." These ideas spread to every teacher training institution in the country and today, are embedded in our early childhood curriculum.

Toward the end of the 19th Century, The Committee of Ten, or Madison Committee, made up of scholars from colleges and administrators from large school districts, met to standardize the curriculum and give it more academic rigor. They set up the modern pattern of academic subjects in the schools and the eight-year sequence of the elementary course and the four-year sequence in secondary schools.

Women's Seminaries

During the 19th Century the most popular magazine for women was *Godi's Women's Magazine*. This publication espoused the "Cult of Domesticity" as it prepared and gave advice on a women's primary occupation as a domestic manager. Many women became teachers and either attended a normal school or a high school with an elective curriculum in pedagogy. However, once a female teacher got married she was expected by custom and tradition to resign and take care of her family. During the 19th Century, pioneering women educators created schools for girls and women that reflected a growing need to educate women beyond the "Cult of Domesticity," and create an academic curriculum for all students. Schools for boys were called academies and schools for girls were called seminaries.

Prudence Crandell started one of the earliest seminaries. In 1831, she started a school for girls in Canterbury, Connecticut. She admitted black students to the school and the people in the town protested, so in 1833, she decided to dedicate the school entirely to the instruction of African-American girls. In 1834, Crandell married a reverend and moved west.

Other reform-minded women built on the idea of academics for women. Prominent among these scholars was Emma Willard who founded the Troy Seminary, in Troy, New York. The Troy institution became famous because it offered college courses for women and opportunities for women teachers. Emma Willard wrote a number of important textbooks including an American History text, which divided the course into two, year-long courses in the history of the United States to and after the Civil War.

Discussion Questions

1. Compare and contrast liberalism and conservatism.
2. Compare and contrast socialism and Marxism.
3. What is nationalism?
4. How did Darwin's ideas impact society?
5. What is Social Darwinism?
6. What were Freud's ideas and how did they affect education?
7. Explain the work of Horace Mann and the rise of the common school movement.
8. What did Henry Barnard do to affect education in America?
9. What was the importance of the Morrill Land Grant Act and the *Kalamazoo Case*?
10. What were normal schools and what was their curriculum like?
11. Discuss the impact of the Committee of Ten.
12. Explain the idea of women's seminaries and the "Cult of Domesticity".
13. Explain the work of Prudence Crandell and Emma Willard.

References & Further Reading

Cubberley, E.P. (1948) *History of education; Educational practice and process considered a phase of the development of western civilization*. New York: Houghton Mifflin

Cuban, L. (1984) *How teachers taught; Constancy and change in classrooms*. New York: Longman.

MacKendrick, P., D. J. Genakoplos, J.H. Hexter, & R. Pipes. (1968) *Western civilization*. New York: Harper and Row

McKay, J. P., B.D. Hill & J. Buckler (1999) *A history of western society*. New York: Houghton Mifflin.

Page, D.P. (1893) *The theory and practice of teaching*. Syracuse: C.W. Bardeen

Chapter 11
The 20ᵗʰ Century and Beyond

Explain the significance of:

People: Benito Mussolini, Giovanni Gentle, Adolph Hitler, Maria Montessori, John Dewey, Woodrow Wilson, Robert LaFollette, Jane Addams, G, Stanley Hall, William H. Kilpatrick, Carelton Washburne, Booker T. Washington, W.E.B. DuBois, Marcus Garvey, Margaret Haley, Helen Parkhurst, Dwight David Eisenhower, Robert Maynard Hutchins, Amos Alonzo Stagg, Mario Salvio, Jimmy Carter, Ronald Reagan, George Bush Sr. William Jefferson Clinton, George Bush Jr.

Terms: progressivism, Hegelian dialectic, 1916 Commission on the Reorganization of Schools, "Cardinal Principles of Education", NAACP, "Atlanta Compromise", accommodationism, confrontationism, NEA, contract method, *Brown v. The Board of Education of Topeka*, Little Rock, Title IX, IDEA, *Engel v. Vital*, *Bakke v. The Board of Regents of the University of California*, Great Books Program, free speech movement, 60s counter-culture, *A Nation at Risk*, *America 2000*, *No Child Left Behind*

European Education

During the 20th Century, education was used as a vehicle to promote nationalism. Italy and Germany in the 20s and 30s developed Fascist states in which education promoted allegiance to the leader. Benito Mussolini's educational advisor, Giovanni Gentile, crafted a curriculum which made the citizen subservient to the state. In Germany, Adolph Hitler developed state-run schools for his elite "supermen." The Soviet Union established a system similar to Hitler's in that good citizens followed their leader. Eventually, most of these countries established schools along the traditional models of the West, which emphasized the role of the individual in a free society. Both England and France constructed educational systems emphasizing modern scientific patterns.

A major European reformer in early childhood education was Maria Montessori. She had a medical degree from the University of Rome. In her practice, Montessori developed a concern for the poor children of Rome. This caused her to develop the Montessori Method of instruction. This method utilized the child's need for tactical stimulation in order to learn the basics of the alphabet. In addition, Montessori realized that children needed child-sized furniture, so it was her innovation to have small chairs and desks, for little children. Early childhood educators everywhere are indebted to her for this improvement alone. Today, there are many Montessori schools all over the world which utilize Montessori's methods and practices to help small children learn.

United States Education

Education in the 20th Century was greatly influenced by John Dewey, the philosopher. Dewey developed an experimental philosophy based on a synthesis of Darwinian evolutionary theory, pragmatism, and the scientific method.
Dewey put his ideas into practice when he became a professor at the University of Chicago. Between 1896 and 1904, he and his wife established, developed and administered a laboratory school for elementary school children. At this site, he utilized a pragmatic educational philosophy as the basis of the children's learning activities.

To Dewey, education was a social process, not an intellectual endeavor. He became identified with the Progressive Education movement and the child-centered school. However, if one looks at Dewey's writings, he was more of a society-centered curriculum theorist rather than a child-centered theorist. Essentially, what Dewey did philosophically was to paint himself into a corner because he set up an Hegelian dialectic, opposing ideas that contradicted each other, with the needs of the child as the thesis (idea) and the needs of society as the antithesis (opposing idea) with the synthesis (new idea) being the school. According to Dewey, if the child's needs are in conflict with the society's needs, the schools most resolve the dilemma in favor of society.

Dewey's ideas were in line with the progressive political leaders of the day such as President Thomas Woodrow Wilson, the reform Governor of Wisconsin, "Fighting" Bob LaFollette, and the leader of the settlement house movement, Jane Addams. Progressivism in education echoed many of the ideals of the political leadership of the age. Key theorists and practitioners were such luminaries as the psychologist philosopher G. Stanley Hall and William H. Kilpatrick, who was a doctoral student of Dewey's. Kirkpatrick implemented the project method of teaching which was a curriculum driven by projects designed to show practical application of school subjects.

The most eminent of educators to put theory into practice was Carelton Washburne. Washburne was the superintendent of schools in Winneka, Illinois in the 1920s. He developed a progressive child-centered curriculum. Washburne was the first to have students switch classes. He introduced shop, physical education and career classes (such as food service) into the high school curriculum. In keeping with the progressive ideology, he was the first to place a pool in the schools, so that students would learn how to swim and to improve their hygiene. If the students swam at least two times a week at least they would be clean and this would contribute to community health.

In 1916, the Committee on the Reorganization of the Schools created a new curriculum for the schools which included social studies. The committee also developed broad objectives for education, which became known as the "Cardinal Principles of Education." These were broad goals for all schools such as reading, writing, and hygiene.

African-American Education

The education of African-Americans changed beginning with the work of Booker T. Washington. Washington believed that blacks could rise to the middle class by becoming teachers. Most schools at this time were segregated and the African-American teachers were in demand to instruct in the black schools. Washington started Hampton Institute and Tuskegee Institute to train teachers and craftsmen. He articulated his views at a meeting of the National Association for the Advancement of Colored People (NAACP) in Atlanta. This speech became known as the "Atlanta Compromise." Washington believed that blacks should not compete with whites for jobs, but learn how to teach and have trades such as a plumbing or carpentry, and as time passed, blacks would increase their standard of living. This approach was known as "accommodationism."

Another black intellectual, W.E.B. Dubois, an eminent historian with a PhD from Harvard, disagreed with Washington. He espoused "confrontationism." DuBois believed that African-Americans should openly compete for jobs with other races. This disagreement radicalized DuBois to such an extent that he became a communist and renounced his U.S. citizenship.

Marcus Garvey was another individual who believed that education was the key to success. Early in the century, he offered blacks correspondence courses in African-American History as well general academic courses in economics and accounting. In the 20th Century, education seemed to be the panacea for most Americans. Blacks and other minorities in the last half of the 20th century have used education as vehicle for advancement in work and society.

Women's Education

In 1901, Margaret Haley was the first women teacher to speak at a general meeting or the National Education Association (NEA). This was extremely significant since 90% of the NEA members were both grade school teachers and women. Three years later, Margaret Haley spoke at the NEA convention in St. Louis, on why teachers should organize. That speech covered problems and issues such as class size and sick leave, which are still debated among teachers' unions today.

Since the beginning of the 20th Century, women reformers began to realize that education was the key to success. More and more women began studying subjects that were primarily the domain of men such areas as history, secondary education, law, medicine and business, because universities finally started to accept women into these courses of study in the middle of the 20th Century.

Among the most prominent women educators of the century was Helen Parkhurst. Parkhurst was a reform pedagogist who developed the contract method of instruction. This method called for the instructor to develop five or six lesson plans and allow the students select the one they wanted to work on. The selection became a contract between student and teacher.

Today, with the passage of legislation and changing attitudes of society, women have made great strides and contributions to American education in both the academic and teaching arenas.

The Impact of the Brown Decision

In the court case of *Brown vs The Board of Education of Topeka Kansas*, the Supreme Court ruled that segregation was illegal. The court believed that "the separate but equal doctrine," which became law in the case of *Plessy vs. Ferguson* was unconstitutional in the area of education. The Justices, in a unanimous decision, stated that separate schools violated the students equal protection rights found in the 14th Amendment.

The full weight of the *Brown* case was brought to bear in Little Rock, Arkansas. The Governor refused to desegregate the schools. President Eisenhower sent in the 101st Airborne to escort the African-American students to school without incident.

As a result, President Johnson introduced the Civil Rights Bill of 1964. This was the first comprehensive civil rights legislation since the Civil War. The Senate filibustered for 88 days at which time the bill became law.

All subsequent inclusion legislation stems from the *Brown* Decision. Important laws that sited *Brown* as a precedent were the Women's Education Equality Act, and Individuals with Disabilities Act (IDEA). The Women's Education Equality Act called for gender equity in educational institutions and the sports programs they operated. This Law was also referred to as Title IX. IDEA or Public Law 94-142, called for students with disabilities to be placed in "the least restricted environment." As a result, every identified special needs student has an IEP or Individual Educational Plan that must be followed by teachers and school districts.

Supreme Court Cases that had an Impact on Education

In addition to the *Brown* decision, a number of court cases over the course of the 20th Century have had a profound impact on education. Among the most interesting cases to led to change in education are *Engel v. Vital* and *Bakke v. The Board of Regents*. In the *Engle* case, the court ruled that Bibles and prayer in public institutions were a violation of the separation of Church and State. The *Bakke* decision involved a middle-aged white male who was denied admission to the University of California Medical School because affirmative action required the institution to select a minority student. The school admitted a black student with lesser credentials than Bakke, so Bakke sued, charging reverse discrimination and court agreed. Bakke had to be admitted to the medical school.

Higher Education

In the area of higher education, the most prominent reformer was Robert Maynard Hutchins, the President of the University of Chicago in the 1920s. The college had the number one football team in the nation coached by the legendary Amos Alonzo Stagg, However, Hutchins eliminated the program because he believed it distracted students from academics. He started the "Great Books Program," and the philosophy of perennialism in education. Hutchins articulated the view that general education in the university should cultivate the intellect. The only way to cultivate the intellect was by reading the "Great Books of Western Civilization," such as Plato's *Republic* and Caesar's *Gallic Wars*. Hutchins stated that the Bachelors degree should be a learner's permit and that students know and understand something only after a graduate education.

In the 1960s, the activist movement on college campuses started at the University of California at Berkley. Mario Salvio and other students began the "Free Speech Movement" in response to the Vietnam War and middle class society in general. This was the beginning of what would become the "counter culture." The 60s counter-culture proved to be a flash in the pan and most 60s radicals today are conservatives.

Presidential Reform

Newspaper reporters once asked President Abraham Lincoln what constituted good education and he replied: "Good education is Horace Mann sitting on a log and a student on the other side!" Lincoln knew that a good teacher was the key to a good education. Through the years, various presidents have made attempts to reform education. This is because no one ever disagrees with them because we all normally want good education. Since most modern presidents were former governors and governors run state educational departments, they feel they have a sound grasp of educational issues.

President Jimmy Carter created the United States Department of Education and made the Secretary of Education a cabinet level appointment. President Ronald Reagan had the first comprehensive assessment of American education known as *A Nation at Risk*. The report stated that public schools were failing and higher academic standards were the remedy for the nation's poor educational situation. This theme of standards was carried into action by President George Bush Sr. in his education summit, *America 2000*. This report called for all schools to reach certain levels of proficiency in basic subjects such as math, science, geography, and English. William Jefferson Clinton, the Governor of Arkansas at the time, was a major author of the report and carried out its recommendations during his eight years as the Chief Executive. President George Bush Jr. led the passage of the *No Child Left Behind Act*. This measure mandated that all children would be successful in school and demanded accountability for teachers and administrators through rigorous testing of both students and teachers. The only segment of the educational community that has never offered any reform program has been the teachers themselves.

Toward the Future

Today, education is under attack from both conservatives and liberals. The future seems to echo past in that curricular reform has given us standards. These national, state, and learned societies statements of what should be taught are the curriculum of the hour. The future also has embraced technology. However, a question must be asked; "Are we using technology to enhance the learning process or are we using it because it is there?"

What will the future hold for education? As long as political leaders hold the purse strings, more accountability, more testing, more standards, and more technology appear to be on the forefront. That being said, the future looks the same as the past, only with more technology. Remember, Lincoln said the best education was: "Horace Mann sitting on a log with a student on the other side!" Good teachers are the key to good education, not computers or standards or tests. An educator who can inspire his or her students to do great things is the essence of the educational process.

Discussion Questions

1. Discuss European education in the 20th Century.
2. Discuss American education in the early 20th Century.
3. Explain African-American education in the 20th Century.
4. Explain Women's education in the 20th Century.
5. What was the impact of the *Brown* Decision on education?
6. Discuss other Supreme Court cases that affected education in the 20th Century.
7. Explain higher education in 20th Century America.
8. Discuss recent presidential educational reforms from Carter to Bush, Jr.
9. Hypothesize educational developments in the future.

References & Further Reading

Bestor, A. (1953) *Educational wastelands*. Urbana: University of Illinois Press.

Cubberley, E.P. (1948) *History of education; Educational practice and process considered a phase of the development of western civilization*. New York: Houghton Mifflin.

Cuban, L. (1984) *How teachers taught; Constancy and change in american classrooms*. New York: Longman.

Curti, M. (1968) *The social ideas of american educators*. Totowa: Littlefield, Adams & Company.

MacKendrick, P., D. J. Genakoplos, J.H. Hexter, & R. Pipes. (1968) *Western civilization*. New York: Harper and Row

McKay, J. P., B.D. Hill & J. Buckler (1999) *A history of western society*, New York: Houghton Mifflin.

Page, D.P. (1893) *The theory and practice of teaching*. Syracuse: C.W. Bardeen

Power, E. J. (1991) *A legacy of learning: A history of western civilization*. Albany: State University of New York Press.

Tindell, G. B. & Shi, D.E. (1999) *America: A narrative history*. New York: W.W Norton & Company.

Wittgenstein, L. (1958) *The blue and brown books* New York: Harper & Row.

Whitehead, A.N. (1929) *The aims of education*. New York: New American Library

Bibliography

Abailard, P. (1976) *Sic et no: A critical edition*. Chicago: University of Chicago Press.

Addams, J. (1985) *Jane addams on education*. New York: Teachers College Press.

Adler, M. (1977) *Philosopher at large: An intellectual autobiography*. New York: Mac-Millan.

Aristotle. (1994) *The complete works of aristotle*. Oxford: Clarendon Press.

Augustine. (1909) *Confessions*. New York: P.F. Collier & Son.

Bacon, F. (1973) *The advancement of learning*. London: Dent

Barnes, A.S.(1885) *Barnes's historical series: A brief history of the united states*. New York: American Book Company.

Bestor, A. (1953) *Educational wastelands: Retreat from learning in our public schools*. Urbana, IL: University of Illinois Press.

Barzun, J. (1991) *Begin here: The forgotten conditions of teaching and learning*. Chicago: University of Chicago Press, 1991.

Brown, P.R.L.(1987) *Augustine of hippo: A biography*. New York: Dorset Press

Butts, F. & L.A. Cremin. (1953) *A history of american education*. New York: Henry Holt.

Cantor, N.F. (2004) *Antiquity: From the birth of sumerian civilization to the fall of rome*. New York: Harper

Cantor, N.F. (1993) *The civilization of the middle ages*. New York: Harper.

Chambliss, J.J. (1971) *Nobility, tragedy, and naturalism: Education in ancient greece*. Minneapolis: Burgess.

Comenius, J.A. (1896) *The great didactic*. London: Adam and Black

Compayre, G. (1888) *History of pedagogy*. Boston: D.C. Heath.

Cremin, L A.(1965) *The wonderful world of ellwood patterson cubberley*. New York: Teachers College.

Cuban, L. (1984) *How teachers taught: Constancy and change in american classrooms*. New York: Longman

Cubberley, E.P. (1948) *History of education: Educational practice and process considered a phase of the development of western civilization*. New York: Houghton Mifflin.

Curti, M. (1968) *The social ideas of american educators.* Totowa: Littlefield, Adams & Company.

Daley, L. J. (1961) *The medieval university.* New York: Sheed & Ward.

Dalton, T. (2002). *Becoming john dewey.* Bloomington: Indiana University Press.

DeGuimps, R. (1896*) Pestalozzi: His life and work.* New York: D. Appleton and Company.

Dewey, J. (1916). *Democracy and education.* New York: MacMillan.

Dewey, J. (1990) *The school and society, the child and the curriculum.* Chicago: University of Chicago Press.

Dunkel, H. B. (1969) *Herbart and education.* New York: Random House.

Dykhuizen, G. (1973). *The life and mind of john dewey.* Carbondale: Southern Illinois University Press.

Froebel, F. (1887) *The education of man.* New York: Appleton.

Gaskoin, C.J.B. (1904) *Alcuin: His life and work.* London: Cambridge University Press.

Good, H.G. (1962) *A history of american education.* Boston: D.C. Heath.

Gutek, G.L. (1995). *A history of the western educational experience.* Prospect Heights: Waveland Press.

Gutek, G.L. (1997) *Philosophical and ideological perspectives on education.* Boston: Allyn and Bacon.

Hamlyn, D. W.(1987) *A history of western philosophy.* New York: Viking Press.

Herbart, J.F. (1901) *Outlines of educational doctrine.* New York: MacMillan.

Herlihy, D. (1970) *The history of feudalism.* New York: Harper Collins.

Herbart, J.F. (1901) *Outlines of educational doctrine.* New York: MacMillan.

Hegel, G.W.RF. (1895) *Lectures on the philosophy of religion.* London: Kegan Paul, Trench, Trubner.

Hutchins, R. M. (1937) *The higher learning in america.* New Haven: Yale University Press

Jackson, P.W. (1998). *John dewey and the lessons of art.* New Haven: Columbia University Press.

Kierkegaard, S. (1983*) Fear and trembling.* Princeton: Princeton University Press.

Kuhn, T. (1957) *The copernican revolution: Planetary astronomy in the development of western thought.* Cambridge: Harvard University Press.

Kuhn, T. (1962) *The structure of scientific revolutions.* Chicago: University of Chicago Press.

MacKendrick, P., D. J. Genakoplos, J.H. Hexter, & R. Pipes.(1968) *Western civilization.* New York: Harper and Row.

Martin, J. M. (2002). *The education of john dewey.* New York: Columbia University Press.

McKay, J. P., B.D. Hill & J. Buckler (1999) *A history of western society.* New York: Houghton Mifflin.

Moore, Paul (1905) *History of education.* New York: MacMillan

Page, D.P. (1893) *The theory and practice of teaching.* Syracuse: C.W. Bardeen

Pestalozzi, J.H. (1951) *The education of man-aphorisms.* New York: Philosophical Library

Plato. (1888) *Republic.* Oxford: Clarendon Press

Power, E. J. (1991) *A legacy of learning: A history of western civilization.* Albany: State University of New York Press.

Quintilian. (1905) *The institutes of oratory.* London: Dewick & Clark.

Stumpf, Samuel.(1999) *Socrates to sartre: A history of philosophy*. 6th ed. New York: McGraw, 1999.

Tanner, D & L. Tanner (1990) *History of the school curriculum*. New York: MacMillan Publishing.

Tarnas, Richard (1991) *The passion of the western mind: Understanding the ideas that have shaped our world view*. NewYork: Ballantine Books.

Tindell, G. B. & Shi, D.E. (1999) *America: A narrative history*. New York: W.W. Norton Company.

Van Doren, Charles (1991). *A history of knowledge: Past, present, and future*. New York: Ballantine Books.

Wagner, D. (1983) *The seven liberal arts in the middle ages*. Bloomington: Indiana University Press.

Walford, E. (1877) *The politics and economics of aristotle*. London: Bell & Dalby.

Westbrook, R.B. (1991). *John dewey and american democracy*. Ithaca: Cornell University Press.

Whitehead, A.N. (1929) *The aims of education*. New York: new American Library

Wittgenstein, L. (1958) *The blue and brown books*. New York: Harper & Row.

Wood, T.E. (2005) *How the catholic church built western civilization*. Washington, D.C.: Regenery Publishing.

Xenophon. (1890) *The works of xenophon*. London: H.G. Dakyns.

Index

About the Author

Mark Mraz is an assistant professor of education at Slippery Rock University of Pennsylvania. He earned a Doctor of Philosophy degree in Curriculum and Instruction with a specialization in Social Studies/History Education from The Pennsylvania State University, a Master of Arts degree in American History as well as a Bachelor of Science in Social Science Education from Indiana University of Pennsylvania. Currently, Mark teaches social studies methods and educational foundations courses at Slippery Rock. Prior to coming to the University, He taught social studies for twenty-nine years at the St Marys Area School District in St. Marys, Pennsylvania. Mark lives in Slippery Rock Pennsylvania with his wife, Sue.

Breinigsville, PA USA
17 May 2010
238195BV00003B/1/P